SHOCKINGLY SUCCESSFUL

Empower Your EMS Vision
*and Transform **Passion** into **Profit***

SHOCKINGLY SUCCESSFUL

Empower Your EMS Vision
*and Transform **Passion** into **Profit***

JEMIMA STEINHART

Niche Pressworks
Indianapolis, IN

For permission to reprint portions of this content or bulk purchases, contact Jemima@EMSMastermind.com

Photo credit: Photo of Natalie and Jemima (chapter 2) Lauren Holub Photography
Icon and design credit: Cora Merriam C. Guevarra
Author photograph by: Lauren Holub Photography

Published by Niche Pressworks; NichePressworks.com
Indianapolis, IN

ISBN
Hardcover: 978-1-962956-45-1
Paperback: 978-1-962956-44-4
eBook: 978-1-962956-46-8

Library of Congress Cataloging-in-Publication Data on File at lccn.loc.gov

This book is dedicated to the entrepreneurs in the EMS (electro-muscle stimulation) field who I have been called to serve: my "EMS Masterminds." You have made it possible for me to do work that I am so passionate about and that I feel is meaningful and worthwhile. This book was created to help you find more answers to how to make your EMS training brand successful and even grow it beyond your wildest dreams. The world needs successful EMS training entrepreneurs to serve more people to achieve their goals with this incredible tool. We are game changers. We are helping people transform to be healthier, fitter, better, faster, and stronger. If this book helps you to reach just one more person and change their life with your God-given gifts, then this work will have been a success. Let's get shockingly successful.

TABLE OF CONTENTS

CREATING A MOVEMENT

RICHARD NEIDLEIN

As a sports scientist with over twenty years of experience in the field of electro-muscle stimulation (EMS) and athletic performance, I have witnessed firsthand how EMS technology is reshaping the way we approach training and rehabilitation. In the ever-evolving world of fitness, few innovations have had such a profound impact, and at the forefront of this revolution is Jemima Steinhart. Her dedication and expertise, combined with the timely release of *Shockingly Successful*, have transformed the way fitness professionals and EMS studio owners approach physical training, offering a fresh perspective on optimizing operations, marketing, and sales.

Jemima's journey with EMS began over fifteen years ago, driven by a passion for harnessing technology to enhance human potential. Her relentless pursuit of excellence and her commitment to sharing her knowledge have made her a respected leader in the industry. Through *Shockingly Successful*, Jemima offers not just a guide but a comprehensive blueprint for success in the EMS field.

This book is a testament to her deep understanding of EMS technology and its applications. It is filled with practical insights, expert interviews, and proven strategies that will empower EMS entrepreneurs, trainers, and enthusiasts alike. Whether you are just starting out or looking to scale your business, Jemima's wisdom and experience will provide you with the tools you need to thrive.

As you delve into the pages of *Shockingly Successful*, you will discover the secrets to unlocking the full potential of EMS. Jemima's clear and engaging writing style makes complex concepts accessible, and her passion for the subject is evident in every chapter. This book is not just about building a business; it is about creating a movement that can change lives.

I am honored to introduce this remarkable work and to celebrate the achievements of a true pioneer in the field. Jemima Steinhart's *Shockingly Successful* is an essential read for anyone serious about making a mark in the world of EMS.

— **Richard Neidlein, MSc,** *certified sports scientist, personal coach, and EMS specialist*

DR. NICK BAUER

Dear Jemima, dear readers,

I am very pleased to write this foreword to *Shockingly Successful* and to have the opportunity to share my experiences and insights from the world of osteopathy, physiotherapy, and electro-muscle stimulation (EMS) with you. I would especially like to express my appreciation for Jemima, a remarkable woman whose energy and passion have been a lasting source of inspiration for me. Our collaboration has shown me the great potential of a dynamic partnership based on innovative methods and mutual trust.

As an osteopath, physiotherapist, and lecturer in holistic medicine, I have developed a unique perspective on the world of training and therapy over the years. This journey has led me to combine traditional approaches with modern technologies like EMS. During my physiotherapy training, I first encountered EMS—a technique that was still in its infancy at the time and primarily used in rehabilitation. Today, EMS has become a mainstay not only in the therapeutic field but also in fitness training and is recognized worldwide.

Meeting Jemima – A Turning Point in Dubai

In 2017, my path led me to Dubai, where I met a remarkable young woman: Jemima. She radiated an infectious energy and passion for movement and training that left a lasting impression. Her expertise in EMS and her innovative approach to training made her an extraordinary partner. From our very first exchange, it was clear that we could achieve great things together.

Through our collaboration, we were able to combine our knowledge and strengths. Her dynamic nature and modern understanding of training techniques complimented my therapeutic expertise perfectly. This allowed us to use EMS effectively both in therapeutic contexts and in regular fitness training, providing our clients with an optimal training experience.

EMS as an Integral Part of Modern Training Concepts

Today, EMS is offered by EMS studios with different concepts around the world, and personal trainers are increasingly using this method to achieve better results for their clients. The benefits are clear: EMS training allows for effective workouts in a short time, strengthens muscles, and simultaneously improves posture. It is especially popular with those seeking new and innovative ways to enhance their fitness.

EMS has also established itself in rehabilitation and pain therapy. Here, we use it to correct muscular imbalances and support recovery after injuries. The versatility of the method makes it an indispensable tool both in the practice of an osteopath and in the gym.

Shockingly Successful – A Valuable Resource for EMS Enthusiasts

Shockingly Successful is an indispensable guide for anyone interested in EMS — whether from a therapeutic, fitness, or athletic perspective. It not only provides an introduction to the fundamental concepts but also offers valuable strategies on how to start your EMS business right.

My Recommendation

For everyone who wants to be successful in the targeted application of EMS, *Shockingly Successful* is a must-read. It is an excellent resource for physiotherapists, trainers, investors, and fitness enthusiasts who want to fully harness the EMS business opportunity. I am convinced that you, whether a beginner or a professional, will benefit from the insights and experiences this book offers.

I wish you the best for your personal development in the EMS field.

— **Nick Bauer, PhD,** *Osteopath, physiotherapist, lecturer in holistic medicine, and CEO of Bauer International Academy of Holistic Medicine (BIAHM)*

THE BOOK I NEEDED

I felt a strong pull to write this book, almost as if the decision was made for me long before I fully realized it. As I looked around the EMS fitness industry, I noticed there was simply **no** book available for EMS training entrepreneurs. Despite the undeniable growth of electro-muscle stimulation (EMS) as a revolutionary training method, those of us trying to build businesses around it were left without a clear roadmap, piecing together information from fitness manuals, marketing books, and trial-and-error experiences.

The fact that there was nothing encouraged me, even though I was insecure at times. Me writing a book? But the purpose is so much bigger than my fear. EMS is so much more than just another fitness trend; it's a technology that can transform lives, offering clients results that traditional training methods can't always achieve in the same time frame. But for those of us who believe in EMS and want to build businesses around it, the path forward isn't always clear. How do you grow an EMS business in a world where many people still don't fully understand what EMS is? How do you market this innovative method, gain client trust, and navigate the ups and downs of running a business that's still new to so many?

This book is my answer to those questions. *Shockingly Successful* is the resource I wish I had when I started — something practical, honest, and focused on the unique challenges EMS entrepreneurs face. I've spent years working in this field, building my own EMS business, and helping others grow theirs. Through those experiences, I've learned what works, what doesn't, and what it takes to build a sustainable business in this evolving industry.

But writing this book wasn't just about filling a gap. It was about answering a calling. I believe EMS has the potential to transform the fitness industry, but more importantly, I believe it can help trainers and business owners create thriving businesses that make a real difference in their clients' lives. That's why I felt compelled to put everything I've learned into these pages — because the tools and strategies for success shouldn't be hidden or scattered. They should be accessible, clear, and actionable.

My goal with *Shockingly Successful* is to guide you through the process of building an EMS business that not only thrives financially, but also delivers lasting value to your clients. Whether you're just starting out or you've been in the EMS industry for years, I hope this book will serve as a practical guide, offering insights and strategies to help you reach the next level.

Thank you for joining me on this journey. I'm excited to share what I've learned, and I can't wait to see the success you create with it.

Let's get started.

— **Jemima Steinhart,** *Founder, Electro Muscle Mastery, EMS Mastermind, my30minutes*

CHAPTER 1

THE EMS MOVEMENT BEGAN IN GERMANY

"You must burn within yourself what you wish to ignite in others."
— **Augustinus von Hippo** *(St. Augustine)*

MY FIRST ENCOUNTER WITH EMS

It was still dark outside when my alarm clock went off at 5:30 a.m. I sat on my bed, rubbing my eyes. "Let's do this again," I thought. I took a deep breath and went to the bathroom in my small basement apartment in Wuppertal-Ronsdorf in Nordrhein Westfalen in Germany. I took a shower, got dressed, picked up my coffee, and got into the car. I drove forty-five minutes to Cologne, where I worked as an office clerk for an IT and telecommunication company from 8:00 a.m. until 4:30 p.m. every day. It would take me another hour and a half to return home because of the afternoon traffic. Despite the long hours, I felt grateful for this career. I had a decent salary, and the company paid for my in-

"You must burn within yourself what you wish to ignite in others."

– Augustinus von Hippo

(St. Augustine)

surance, car, and phone. But I just couldn't imagine doing this my whole life. I was also about to finish my bachelor's degree in economics. I'd study in the evenings, through the nights, and on weekends. I was dedicated, but there was no passion. I wanted more. I wanted to do something more purposeful.

Growing up in a dysfunctional family was hard. My parents fought all the time. It was loud and verbally, emotionally, and physically abusive at home. I struggled with allergies, eating disorders, and social anxiety. I was constantly bullied, and I suffered a lot during my school years. It got better when I started working and left home. At this point in my life, I felt I had conquered a different milestone for myself. I was always seeking to break the cycle — to break out of the generational trauma and hurt of my parents and grandparents — so I sought help to do better. I started to eat healthier and maintain a healthier weight. I went to a little Power Plate (vibration plate) studio where I received personal training, and I was running three times a week. My main struggle was always to maintain a balance, to not go to extremes, even with exercising. I loved fitness and anything that had to do with living healthier and fitter. It was my newfound passion. The idea grew more and more in my mind: What if I could change my career and instead of working in an office, I could open a personal training studio to help people transition into their dream bodies and dream fitness level? What if I could do what I am most passionate about all day?

I wanted to learn more about the fitness industry, so I signed up for a Level 2 training program and delved deeper into nutrition with a multilevel supplement company, where I began consulting customers on weight loss options.

At this point, I didn't know that I was about to find out about an electro-muscle stimulation suit that would turn my life upside down and change everything.

A couple of weeks later, I met an acquaintance at a nutrition supplement marketing event. We were just hanging out after the presentation when she started talking. "Jemima, in my gym in Haan, they have these new devices."

"What is it?" I asked.

"It's called electro-muscle stimulation. You wear a full-body suit that stimulates all your muscles, and then you train with it for twenty minutes with a personal trainer."

"Wait, what?!"

"Yes, they make you wear this black underwear under it, and it feels really weird. Aren't you looking into tools right now for your thing you want to do?" (I had told her about my dream of having a boutique personal training studio.)

"Can I try it out?"

"Yes, sure. I'll send you all the information."

"Awesome, thanks."

I contacted the gym and booked a trial session. Off I was on my way to Haan, another little city not far from Wuppertal. Was this the thing I had been waiting for? I don't know why, but I always had this expectation inside of me, that something was waiting to be my longed-for purpose in my professional life. I stepped into this big gym, and the receptionist showed me the way to a separate section where two guys were working. One of them introduced himself to me and handed me a pack of long-sleeved underwear. "You can change over there. Just wear the underwear and nothing under it."

"Okay. Nothing under it? No underwear?" I felt super nervous. *What is about to happen? Is it going to hurt?* My anticipation grew. *How is this going to feel?*

"Okay," I nodded. I changed super fast. I was ready for this new experience, as if I knew my life was about to change forever. I felt excited but tense. He helped me into the suit and showed me how to get into a basic position, pre-tense my body, and start leveling up the intensity. I felt the current stimulating all my larger muscle groups, along with areas that I never felt before in my body. While he instructed me to do different basic exercises like lunges and squats, my head was already racing. This was it. This was it. After finishing my trial session, I drove home.

SLEEPLESS NIGHTS

It was raining (as it often did in Wuppertal), and the windshield wipers were going fast — almost as fast as my pounding heart. This was it! I had found a tool that was going to change my life and the lives of millions, maybe even billions, of people. I couldn't sleep for the next three nights. Sitting at my kitchen table, all the ideas I had for creating a personal training lounge came together. What do I call it? Twenty-five-minute workout? Thirty-minute workout? I researched and saw that there was already someone using twenty-five minutes. Then I thought, *Well, twenty minutes is the EMS session, five minutes is the relaxation, and in five minutes they change. That's 30 minutes...* but the domain was taken, damn it! I thought more. *In the end, it's going to be "my time, my EMS workout, and my transformation," so my30minutes it is...* This was it. I found it!

Little did I know what was about to come. Little did I know how long this journey would take and how much pain I would go through.

That feeling of being excited and scared at the same time never left me. I had just finished my Level 2 certification and drove to Munich, sick with a 40-degree fever (104 degrees Fahrenheit), to do my Level 3 workshop — certifying me as a personal trainer to be able to train people one-on-one with EMS. I was terrified. How would I get the ten clients I'd need to at least cover my expenses? How would I get a studio? How would I pay my bills? I had to leave my job. Leave my financial stability and all the certainty I had at this point in my life.

I needed a business plan. When I had a business plan, I could go to the bank and present it, and everything would be fine, or so I thought. Looking back, I don't know why I was so sure I would get a loan without a problem. Oh, how wrong I was. However, I wrote my first EMS training business plan.

NO LOAN!

It was Monday morning, and I was sitting in the bank office with Frau Marcus. She was in her late forties and, let's put it this way, didn't look like someone who prioritizes health and fitness. She didn't offer me any water or coffee. Another lady from the loan department was there. They asked me a lot of questions.

"So, Frau Steinhart, you are planning to open an EMS studio where you intend to sell ten EMS training classes for 500 euros?"

"Yes, that's right, ma'am."

The whole questioning lasted over ninety minutes. I was in my element, talking my heart and soul out. But I was talking against a wall, and my mouth dried out. Still, no water was offered. "The thing is, Frau Steinhart, nobody knows what EMS is, and we don't believe you will achieve the numbers projected in your business plan. We are sorry to deny your request, but we wish you..." Blah, blah, blah.

My throat swelled. My heart and stomach dropped. I was so freaking disappointed. I walked out crying. Back in my apartment, I just wanted to bury myself under the blanket. OMG. This would never work. And at this point I had already left my job. What was I going to do? My friend encouraged me. "You need to go to all the other banks in town. One will certainly give you a loan." So, I sent my business plan to all the other banks in my town. It took weeks. It was Christmastime, and they were all on vacation. The next bank said no. The next one said no, the next one... I was so down. I read the story of the Kentucky Fried Chicken founder, Colonel Sanders, who was rejected dozens of times until finally, one bank said yes. I cried, went to bed, woke up, and tried another one.

One day, I had my dad on the phone. He asked me, "What's happening?" "Ach, Dad, I don't think it's going to work out. I better just apply for another job before my money runs out."

"How much do you need?" he asked.

"I was asking for fifty thousand euros, but I can start with 25K minimum if I only start with one EMS machine and a little bit of decorating for the place."

"I'm sorry, child, but I can't give you this money."

We hung up. Yet another day when I just wanted to bury my head under the blanket. The next day, my phone rang. It was my dad again.

"You said you need a minimum of 25K?"

"Yes, actually 23K. If I just do the bare minimum, I'll need around 15K to buy one EMS machine with the initial set of vests. The remaining amount will be used to renovate the studio, build a front desk, install showers, paint the studio, and buy some lounge furniture and items for the changing rooms."

"Okay, look, it's my and your mum's retirement fund, but I believe in you and your project, so I'll transfer it to you."

"Really?"

I felt a mix of relief and responsibility in my stomach. This was the answer to my problem and such a big burden at the same time. A huge responsibility. The next day, I had the money in my account, and I placed the order for my first EMS machine.

My journey had just begun.

ONE EMS MACHINE AND A LEAP OF FAITH

The good news was I was about to change the world with my EMS machine and my idea of how I would transform people with the my30minutes concept. But the bad news was I had no idea how to run an EMS training business.

Here I was, with one EMS machine, one little studio, and eight thousand euros left to make this work. No savings. My siblings were unhappy about my dad giving me that money. There was concern and jealousy at the same time.

I walked a friend through my new place. It didn't look like a boutique gym yet, but I tried to draw the picture. "And here will be the consulting area, and here we are building another shower."

"Wait," my friend said. "You are planning to do what?" I could see the disbelief in their eyes. I had seen this before. The memory of Frau Marcus from the bank came into my mind. *Ughhhh, is everyone really against me? Against this?* My boyfriend, who was pursuing his own network marketing career, was no help either once he learned that this studio wasn't just there to sell his products and sign people up into his network. We ended up breaking up shortly after my opening. But I was convinced this would work. This would impact people's lives.

I remember how I was counting my expenses. Monthly rent. Electricity. Utilities. I had this little profit and loss spreadsheet and remembered that I would need ten clients to break even. I had a couple of long nights calculating it up and down and asking myself over and over: *Will I be able to onboard ten clients?* Every time my mind wanted to wander and panic, I told myself: *If it's not working, I can just get employed again.* That's it. And I wrote lists. Lists of anyone I knew who I could invite for an EMS trial session.

With the help of my friends, I painted the studio. I bought items for the changing room and built a studio front desk/bar. I got a cross-trainer and some dumbbells, mirrors for the walls, and booked my first article in the local newspaper. Facebook was really just to connect with friends from school, and there was no Instagram. I had a little notebook with a calendar, and I would tell everyone about EMS and start booking trial sessions. I let everyone pay a minimum fee for the trial. My little savings were gone, and there was no salary coming in. I tried to book the appointments back to back so I could come into the studio for appointment blocks.

SOLO ENTREPRENEURSHIP

I had a little body composition scale, a measurement tape, and a basic intake form. I offered a ten-session card, one-year and two-year memberships, weekly and twice-weekly sessions. I was the trainer, the salesperson, the receptionist, and the cleaner. I became part of a business network like BNI that met weekly for breakfast. It was super uncomfortable. But that's where I learned to do an elevator pitch. I sold my first membership to Thomas B., who lost twenty-five kilos in his first year. He brought me his wife, and she brought me her family and friends, and they brought me more referrals. Thomas and his wife are still in my life today, and I love them deeply as they've walked this journey together with me.

DEBT-FREE AND FULL CAPACITY

I didn't just sign up ten clients in three months. I signed up over one hundred clients, and I paid my dad back in full. I grew so rapidly that within a few months, I had over 150 memberships. That is what this book is about. To teach you everything you need to have a highly profitable and successful EMS training studio.

I had to buy another machine, and soon, my first intern, Dominik, walked into my EMS studio and said: "My aunt trains with you. I want to work with you." So he did. He was fifteen years old at the time, first being my intern, then my trainee, and then my first EMS trainer. He stayed loyal to me for years. God bless you always, Dominik.

My clients started seeing results, losing twenty pounds, thirty pounds, sixty pounds, and yes, even 120 pounds. I found a program with EMS that worked. I combined EMS strength training with EMS cardio sessions. I held my clients accountable and gave basic nutrition advice. I sold supplements (protein shakes, vitamins, fat burners, BCAAs). I weighed and measured clients regularly to upsell the ones who came once a week to two times a week, and grew my first team. I started semi-private group EMS classes with three, then four people. I worked hard every single day, including Saturdays and sometimes Sundays. I got my license so I could employ trainees to become sports and fitness merchants. I had part-time trainers and students, and I loved my work.

There was nothing I loved more than a satisfied customer after an amazing EMS session. I cherished the conversations we had during and after the sessions. The most important thing was for me to continuously educate my clients about the benefits of EMS training. I focused on always having this as the main conversation, which led to more referrals.

Another secret of my success was that selling became easy when I knew I could transform my clients' lives and build another ambassador for EMS training. I loved that I was doing something different. I loved proving my doubters wrong, showing that this was working and my clients were seeing results.

My first year (2010) as an EMS studio owner with my clients Jana (r.), Nora, and Max

I trained enthusiastically with EMS myself. I wore the suit, using the metabolic program on the cross-trainer, sweat dripping down my forehead. I looked outside the window. I wasn't done yet. This wasn't it. I had big ambitions. I remembered telling the banks that rejected me, "If this model works in Wuppertal, a 300,000-citizen town with high unemployment, it can work all over the world. This could be the future McDonald's franchise of fitness." I wouldn't stop. I needed to go out into the world and grow this opportunity. This was a win-win-win situation for everyone. The studio owners would win, the trainers would win, and the clients would win.

I daydreamed about getting more exposure and about the US market. I remember my dad once coming back from a mission trip to Atlanta, Georgia, bringing a jar of peanut butter. I can't really tell you why, but I was always drawn to the big American dream by people who believed in bigger dreams and goals. Meanwhile, I was listening to Tony Robbins (author, speaker, and coach) in my car, whenever I could. My customers would complain about the weather. Well, I had to admit, the weather in West Germany was pretty dreary most of the time. Imagine cold, rainy, wet, dark weather most of the year, with a few summer days in spring and summer, but that's it. I knew that EMS was going to grow and that more people would discover it and see the opportunities in it.

I hired my first coach in franchising and worked on my documents and business plan. At this point, I already had two EMS machines, so I bought a third and started offering group training. I also did concierge services (training customers in the comfort of their homes) for nine hundred euros per ten sessions. I expanded my first EMS brand into countries like the United Arab Emirates, Qatar, Jordan, and the United States. I opened up and ran ten EMS studios and multiple franchises, and I distributed EMS equipment.

The point I want to make is that you, too, can fill your studio with paying clients and be highly profitable using this formula. Today, I help EMS entrepreneurs all over the world build EMS businesses the smart way with automated sales, marketing, certification, onboarding, and operational systems. I teach sales and marketing for the EMS niche. I help my customers pre-qualify their clients, trainers, and partners and look into what drives them to make healthy, sustainable decisions. I own my story — the triumphs and the trials — and share it with others as I see how that transparency benefits others in my mentorship and consultation programs.

Where are you on your EMS training journey, are you just starting to plan? Have you received your EMS equipment and just started to design your first studio? Do you already have one or multiple studios? Is your vision to build an EMS franchise? Wherever you are, it doesn't really matter. This book is for you!

Save your time to spend with your loved ones and avoid all the mistakes I've made. If you're feeling frustrated because you're not getting enough leads, your retention rates are low, or you don't know how to find the right trainers so you can step back a little, trust me when I say I know how you feel. I've been there, and in this book, I will walk you through the steps to get out of the valley.

KEY LESSONS

In my first years as an EMS entrepreneur, I went through a series of valuable lessons that shaped how I approach my business today. Here's how I walked through these lessons:

1. **My vision is uniquely mine, and I must stay committed to it.** Early on, I realized that my vision was something deeply personal. No one else could understand it

in the same way I did, and no one had the right to take it away. I had to stay committed to my dream, even when others didn't share my enthusiasm or see my potential. I told myself, "No matter what, I will stay committed to my dream."

2. **Focus on your "why" instead of the "how."** When I started, I was often caught up in trying to figure out every small detail of how things would work. Over time, I understood that if my "why" was big and strong enough, the "how" would reveal itself. It wasn't about obsessing over the process, but staying focused on the purpose behind what I was doing. I often reminded myself, "I am in the process of achieving my dream outcome."

3. **It's okay to lose people along the way.** I quickly learned that not everyone would understand or support my journey, and that was fine. There were moments when I felt alone or doubted myself, but I had to remind myself not to fall into negative thinking. I let go of people who couldn't see my vision and focused on those who did.

4. **Prioritize your dream customer and deliver results fast.** I also realized that to truly succeed, I needed to be loyal to my customers. Their success was my success. I focused on providing fast, tangible results that would improve their lives, even if it meant putting in extra work. By staying loyal to my dream customers, I built trust and a solid foundation for my business.

5. **Understand what drives you.** There were times I struggled with feeling burnt out, thinking I needed to be everything to everyone. Over time, I learned that false ambition is toxic. It was crucial for me to understand my own motivation and drive and to distinguish that from external pressures. Understanding what really fueled me kept me from burning out.

6. **Set healthy boundaries with customers and employees.** One of the hardest lessons was learning to say no. At first, I was afraid to disappoint people, but I quickly realized that setting boundaries was necessary for both my business and my well-being. Healthy boundaries helped me maintain balance and prevent burnout, and I was better able to serve both my customers and my team.

They say an overnight success takes a decade. Well, this is my second decade, so I've saved you one. With the knowledge and experience I've gained, you will be able to achieve success and help your dream clients get the results they wish for with the most amazing tool available in the fitness and health industry: electro-muscle stimulation.

Let's get started.

CHAPTER 2

THE EMS OPPORTUNITY

THE BURDEN OF Dis-EASE

Growing up, I saw a lot of suffering created by coping mechanisms rooted in past trauma. I watched my dad eating his feelings. After the war in Germany, my grandmother was alone with five kids to raise and worked non-stop to make a living. My grandfather drank himself to death after he returned. He weighed just eighty pounds, having spent seven years in work camps, first in Ukraine, then in the USA. My grandmother gave her kids chocolate as a substitute for love; that was her love language during times when she worked tirelessly and nearly died from ovarian cancer, later suffering from diabetes. Baffled by the war, work and sugar were all she had left to survive.

I witnessed all this — the suffering of my parents, the suffering of my grandparents — and made it my responsibility in life not only to study it but to recover from this generational hurt. I personally believe we are a generation that is more aware, more conscious of what is happening, and ready to break the generational trauma. It doesn't matter if it was started by war, like my heritage. I just know that the diseases we see today in our society have a root, and that I can't be alone in wanting to help cure it.

This personal experience became one of my greatest motivators. From a young age, I not only sought help for myself but also explored ways to adopt a healthier diet and engage in regular exercise. Exercising has become a newfound tool to not only regulate myself but also to keep me healthier. I was determined to make a difference and assist others in their journey toward a healthier lifestyle. Little did I know that electro-muscle stimulation would become my vehicle to help people of all kinds overcome their personal challenges and become healthier, stronger, fitter, and better. The graphic below shows that it was not only a personal matter but that our society suffers from the burden of these diseases.

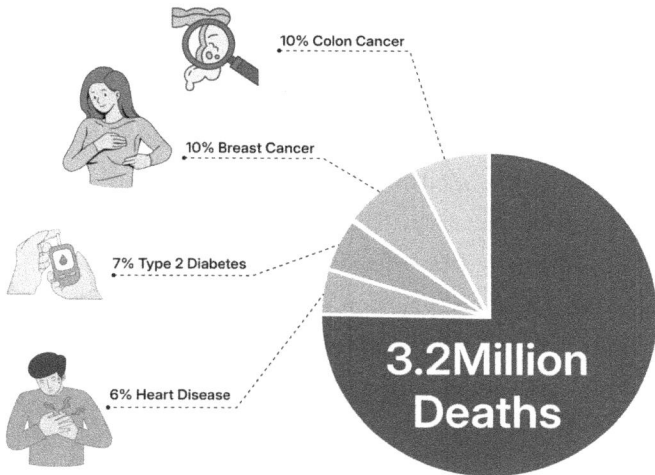

10% Colon Cancer

10% Breast Cancer

7% Type 2 Diabetes

6% Heart Disease

3.2Million Deaths

Physical inactivity is linked to around 3.2 million deaths annually worldwide, according to the World Health Organization (WHO)[1].

THE IMPACT OF PHYSICAL INACTIVITY ON PUBLIC HEALTH

Physical inactivity is a global concern that contributes to the prevalence of non-communicable diseases such as cardiovascular diseases, cancer, and diabetes. The World Health Organization reports that approximately 25% of adults and 81% of adolescents worldwide do not meet the recommended guidelines for physical activity. This alarming statistic has significant economic implications. Studies have shown that physical

---

1   World Health Organization, "Global Recommendations on Physical Activity for Health," World Health Organization, 2010, https://www.who.int/publications/i/item/9789241599979.

inactivity costs the global economy around $67.5 billion annually in healthcare expenditures and lost productivity[2].

The WHO statistics are alarming: approximately 3.2 million deaths annually are linked to physical inactivity. Among the leading causes of death worldwide is heart disease, often stemming from factors such as high blood pressure, high cholesterol, unhealthy lifestyles, unhealthy diet, stress, using alcohol, drugs, and prescription drugs, and smoking. These key contributors to heart disease and other medical conditions are frequently associated with poor lifestyle choices, including obesity and diabetes.

REVERSING DISEASE

To put it simply, living an unhealthy lifestyle without regular training and proper nutrition significantly increases the risk of these diseases.[3] However, I firmly believe that with the help of electro-muscle stimulation (EMS) training, we can reverse these detrimental lifestyle patterns. By implementing a manageable

---

2 Institute for Health Metrics and Evaluation (IHME), "Global Burden of Disease Study 2017 (GBD 2017) Results," IHME, University of Washington, 2017, http://ghdx.healthdata.org/gbd-results-tool.

3 I.M. Lee, E. J. Shiroma, F. Lobelo, P. Puska, S. N. Blair, and P. T. Katzmarzyk. "Effect of Physical Inactivity on Major Non-Communicable Diseases Worldwide: An Analysis of Burden of Disease and Life Expectancy." *The Lancet* 380, no. 9838 (2012): 219-29, https://doi.org/10.1016/S0140-6736(12)61031-9;Institute for Health Metrics and Evaluation (IHME), "Global Burden of Disease Study 2017 (GBD 2017) Results," IHME, University of Washington, 2017, http://ghdx.healthdata.org/gbd-results-tool; Peter T Katzmarzyk and I-Min Lee. "Sedentary Behaviour and Life Expectancy in the USA: A Cause-Deleted Life Table Analysis," *BMJ Open* 2, no. 4 (2012), e000828. https://doi.org/10.1136/bmjopen-2012-000828.

training routine and gradually fostering accountability, we can support individuals in making healthier choices.

Additionally, integrating nutrition guidance tailored to our clients can further enhance their journey toward better health. EMS training provides an effective means to not only improve physical fitness but also to instill sustainable habits that contribute to overall well-being.

HOPE

Regular physical activity can reduce the risk of heart disease, stroke, diabetes, and various types of cancer by up to 30%.[4] With our EMS system, we provide one of the most supportive, safest, and easiest ways for individuals to increase their physical activity levels.

Our purpose in this business goes beyond establishing a successful enterprise; it lies in being a game changer and a transformational helper. By offering EMS training, we have the power to change people's lives in a literal sense. While many may not yet realize their need for it, the numbers and statistics underline the importance of our purpose.

Seizing the Opportunity

As an EMS studio owner, you find yourself in an opportune position. The fitness and health market is undergoing a shift,

---

4 Centers for Disease Control and Prevention, "Physical Activity and Health," last modified 2021, https://www.cdc.gov/physicalactivity/basics/pa-health/index.htm.

with people becoming more educated about the importance of fitness and wellness. Simultaneously, the prevalence of chronic diseases necessitates effective solutions for maintaining a healthy lifestyle. By capitalizing on this growing market, you have the chance to be part of a movement that will be remembered as a turning point in the industry.

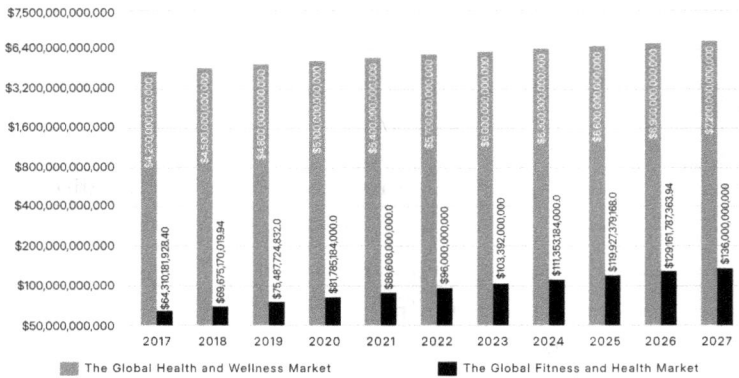

Fig. 1. The growing fitness and wellness market.

Implications for the Future

Given the significant health benefits and the efficiency of EMS training, it presents a promising solution for addressing the growing health issues in a sedentary society. Its appeal spans a wide demographic, including older adults and individuals with limited capacity for conventional exercise. The positive outcomes in terms of strength, body contouring, mood, and overall health suggest that EMS could play a crucial role in preventive health strategies and therapeutic interventions. This is your chance to position yourself to be part of a growing market.

Testimonials and Experiences: Sharing Real-Life Success Stories and Personal Transformations

In May 2002, my fitness life changed forever. I was diagnosed with breast cancer, had a bilateral mastectomy, and had breast reconstruction with a TRAM flap. That means that they cut my rectus abdominis. Since then, I have struggled to be able to meet any of my fitness goals. When I lost that muscle connection, I lost my ability to concentrate on a muscle group and activate it during exercise. I am currently sixty and postmenopausal. Fast-forward to April 2023, when I met Natalie Hussion. She's the CEO and founder of EMS Enhanced in Houston, Texas. My awesome Pilates instructor introduced us to up my game, help my mind muscle connection, strengthen my core, and increase my balance. That is exactly what has happened! Every bit of it is like a dream come true. I feel muscles that I haven't felt in twenty-two years. I am building muscle, changing shape, regaining balance, and I actually have a core (oblique and transverse) to strengthen now!

EMS training has changed my life. I stay so much more energized and strong.

Natalie (Founder EMS Enhanced) will tell you: Nothing comes between me and my EMS!

— *Kelly Walters*

INDUSTRY INSIGHTS

EMS Enhanced: The Journey of Natalie Hussion, CEO and Founder

Before embarking on her EMS (electro-muscle stimulation) training business journey, Natalie Hussion spent fifteen years as a business development and brand manager in corporate America. She had a successful career, continually advancing and gaining exceptional experience that would later propel her toward entrepreneurship. Despite her professional success, Natalie felt her skills were underutilized, and her passion for her career was waning.

When Everything Changed

In addition to feeling not seen enough in her career, the world was also confronted with a pandemic that took corporate America and the world on an unforeseen journey with many unknowns. The typical nine-to-five office life became work-from-home.

During her time at home, for the first time in her career, she experienced a true work-life balance and was able to be more involved in her daughter's life. While adjusting to her "new normal," her family also received the devastating news that Natalie's mother was diagnosed with a rare neurodegenerative disease called Creutzfeldt-Jakob disease that has no cure and only a small window of time before the inevitable death. "When you are faced with two out-of-control situations — a pandemic and your mother's foreseeable death — you take a step back and reflect on what is really important in life," Natalie says. Her career, which had moved her across the country from Wisconsin to Texas, was no longer her priority. Her time with her family became of utmost importance.

Enough is Enough

With her mother's passing and the realization that life was too short to spend on unfulfilling work, Natalie decided to quit her corporate job and start her EMS training business journey. She was initially introduced to EMS as a consumer and fell in love with the results, the technology, and the potential it held for the general population in health and wellness. Her goal was to help others feel good about themselves and achieve optimal fitness results efficiently through EMS training.

"The goal I wanted to achieve by starting my EMS company was to help others feel good about themselves and introduce a new way to achieve optimal fitness results in an efficient manner," Natalie further explains. "My spin on EMS is 'efficient, motivation, synergy' because that is exactly what the training is. Both your time spent and the results received are efficient, the endorphin release is the best motivation, and the synergy between the EMS technology and the human body is a powerful force," Natalie shares.

Lack of Awareness for EMS

Starting the EMS business came with its own set of challenges. The biggest obstacle for Natalie was public disbelief and lack of awareness about EMS. Most people confused it with emergency medical services. Natalie faced skepticism and had to continually educate clients and the general public about what EMS truly was and its benefits. Additionally, the business required her to juggle multiple roles — EMS trainer, IT specialist, equipment expert, and program manager — all while managing her time effectively to maintain a work-life balance.

"After I purchased my equipment, I asked my distributor questions regarding the science behind EMS, read white paper studies, and wanted to deep dive into being the best personal trainer in the field equipped with extensive knowledge in electro-muscle stimulation/electrophysiology. That is when my distributor introduced me to you, Jemima, and to your approach. I was instantly interested, and after our first call, I signed up first to become an EMS master trainer and then for monthly consulting services to help my business flourish," she explains.

"It gave me confidence that I had the best in the field on standby to help as issues arose in the field, and trust me, you will run into several odd occurrences — between clients' ailments, off-the-cuff questions about EMS, and equipment issues. Not only are you the EMS trainer, but you are also the IT specialist, the equipment expert, and the overall program manager. I felt confident that if I could not instantly provide a solution to a client as a need arose, I could consult Jemima, and we would be able to provide the client with what they needed in a quick turnaround time. Customer service is of utmost importance to me, and Jemima also embodies that quality. She is truly a breath of fresh air. Not only is she hardworking and a pillar of institutional EMS knowledge, but she is a devoted wife and mother. I admire and look up to her as a role model," Natalie says.

Turning Point

The partnership with Jemima and EMS Mastermind provided Natalie with the tools and confidence to excel as an EMS trainer. With Jemima's support, Natalie organized the first USA EMS Expert Panel event, further establishing herself as a leader in the EMS community.

"The list could go on and on, but the key elements are these: the science behind EMS, contraindications explained in full detail, and the white paper studies. That is the institutional knowledge that you cannot get from a distributor, and as an EMS professional, you need to be equipped with it in the field in order to succeed. The distributor is great for equipment issues specific to their brand, but outside of that, you need to find an expert, like Jemima, to team up with to help you and your trainers really embrace and understand EMS and how to properly administer it in the field for both safety and results," Natalie emphasizes.

Today, Natalie runs a successful EMS training business and brand licenses her EMS know-how. She enjoys more flexibility and time with her family, no longer constrained by the rigid structure of corporate life. Her journey has been filled with challenges, but the rewards have been immense. She has built a community of EMS champions and continues to educate and inspire others. Her business not only helps people achieve their fitness goals but also transforms lives. Natalie's story is a testament to taking leaps of faith, embracing new paths, and the incredible potential of EMS training.

Reflecting on her journey, Natalie shares, "Still trying to establish a work-life balance, but it has been a fun journey, and

I do have more time to spend with my family and the flexibility to schedule time off when I would like. No more PTO days!"

Natalie Hussion (left), Founder EMS Enhanced, and me :)

As we embark on this journey in the EMS training industry, let us remember the profound impact we can make on the lives of millions or billions of people. By addressing the global issue of physical inactivity, we have the opportunity to improve public health and increase the quality of life for individuals worldwide. Join us as we embrace our purpose and strive to create a positive change in the world through EMS training. We are realizing now that we are game changers, that we have a real opportunity to make a difference, and that we have a place in a growing market.

If you would like to learn more about the EMS brand license opportunity, scan the QR code:

INDUSTRY INSIGHTS FROM DR. NICK BAUER

In recent years, I've closely observed the shifts in our society, and it's evident that our way of living has changed significantly. Many people's daily routines are dominated by long hours of sitting, high levels of stress, and an increasingly digital work environment. This lifestyle has profound effects on our physical health, leading to widespread issues like lack of movement, muscle tension, and chronic pain due to neglect of essential muscle activity.

This is where I see the importance of a consistent, long-term health routine and why I believe that electro-muscle stimulation (EMS) holds such great potential. EMS offers a way to activate deep muscle groups that are often missed by conventional training methods. It's an efficient solution that fits seamlessly into the modern lifestyle, even for those who are short on time. With EMS, people can strengthen their muscles and improve circulation effectively, all while maintaining a busy schedule.

Synergies Between EMS, Osteopathy, and Traditional Training

One of the most valuable insights from my work with Jemima was how effectively EMS can be combined with other approaches. The combination of EMS and osteopathic techniques offers significant benefits in both training and pain therapy. While osteopathic treatment aims to understand the body as a whole and to resolve blockages and dysfunctions, EMS allows for targeted muscle strengthening and activation of muscle groups that are often neglected in traditional exercises.

This synergy is evident, for example, in working with people who want to improve their performance without overloading their joints. With EMS, we can target specific muscle groups, while osteopathic treatment ensures that movements remain balanced and harmonious. People with chronic pain also benefit from this combination, as EMS offers them a gentle way to activate their muscles and support the healing process without putting unnecessary strain on the body. One of the most memorable cases that comes to mind is from my time working in Dubai. There, I worked with an entrepreneur who had suffered from severe back pain for years, largely due to his sedentary work habits and poor posture at the office. Traditional treatment approaches provided only temporary relief, as his demanding career left little room for regular physical therapy or fitness sessions. By combining targeted osteopathic techniques with EMS training, we were able to strengthen his deep back muscles and improve his range of motion. Within just a few months, he experienced a significant reduction in pain, alongside noticeable improvements in his overall fitness and posture.

This case continues to remind me of the critical importance of sustainable health routines that align with our modern lifestyles. EMS isn't just a tool for athletes or therapists; it's a practical solution for anyone seeking an effective way to maintain their health over the long term. It bridges modern technology with traditional approaches to physical therapy. If we can integrate EMS consistently into our lives, we can better counteract the physical impacts of a demanding, fast-paced life and significantly enhance our quality of life."

— **Nick Bauer, PhD,** *Osteopath, physiotherapist, lecturer in holistic medicine, and CEO of Bauer International Academy of Holistic Medicine (BIAHM)*

Learn more about BIAHM:

Scan me!

Ready to Take Your EMS Business to the Next Level?

What does it really take to not only build an EMS business but also create a brand that stands out and becomes a household name in the industry? In the next chapter, we'll break down the essential steps to establish a thriving EMS studio and strategies to make your brand unforgettable. Let's dive into the proven methods that will transform your vision into reality.

Stay with me — you won't want to miss this!

CHAPTER 3

THE SECRET TO MARKETING EMS TRAINING

TRIALS AND ERRORS

EMS training is still not well-known. People simply don't know that they want it. If they did, they would be running to EMS training studios and screaming, "Sign me up!" Sometimes, this is the expectation that new EMS training studios and business owners have. I remember that feeling, and I still feel it — having found a gem, a tool that changes people's lives, and just wanting to tell everyone about it. Here's the problem: People haven't had the same experience as you. In fact, they haven't had any experience with electro-muscle stimulation (EMS) training at all, so they can't know that they want it.

Promoting EMS by itself was definitely a trial-and-error process. People simply don't get excited by something they don't know because they can't see what's in it for them. In the early days, suppliers would tell us (new customers, studio owners) that EMS is for everyone! Specifically, for everyone who doesn't have time. But fifteen years in, I can tell you that *no one* has time for fitness training. And no one has money. When things get a little tight economically, what is the first thing people cut out? Did you say their EMS training? That's right. The first thing they cut is anything that they struggle to do by themselves to begin with. And this is — most of the time — something related to their health and is not a quick fix. We saw the evidence in chapter 2 of how this impacts their health.

Early marketing efforts looked like this: I would highlight the time aspect, that it's "only twenty minutes," and promote the supplier's equipment and the promised benefits of the technology (how convenient for them, lol). I would describe its safety aspect and benefits, such as:

Efficiency and Convenience: EMS training can achieve significant results in a shorter amount of time compared to traditional workouts. A twenty-minute EMS workout is comparable to a ninety-minute workout in a traditional gym.

Muscle Activation: EMS targets deep muscle fibers that are often difficult to engage with conventional exercises, activating fast-twitching fibers from the start (Henneman's principle revert).[5]

5 Henneman's Principle, also referred to as the Size Principle, was introduced by Dr. Elwood Henneman in the 1950s. It describes the sequential recruitment of motor units based on the intensity of the required force. Low-threshold

Improved Strength: Regular EMS training can enhance muscle strength and endurance.

Enhanced Recovery: EMS can aid in muscle recovery and reduce post-workout soreness.

Increased Metabolism: The intensity of EMS training can boost metabolism, aiding in weight management, due to higher calorie consumption within the training period and the afterburn effect.

Reduced Risk of Injury: EMS training is low-impact, making it suitable for those recovering from injuries or with joint issues.

Customizable Workouts: EMS can be tailored to individual fitness levels and goals.

Posture Improvement: By strengthening core and back muscles, EMS can help improve posture.

Rehabilitation Support: EMS is often used in physical therapy to support muscle rehabilitation and prevent atrophy.

---

motor units containing smaller, fatigue-resistant slow-twitch muscle fibers are recruited first for low-intensity activities. As the demand for force increases, high-threshold motor units containing larger, fast-twitch muscle fibers are progressively recruited. This orderly recruitment pattern ensures energy efficiency and smooth muscle function during various physical activities (Henneman et al., 1965). The principle has significant implications for neuromuscular training and rehabilitation, as it underpins the rationale for progressively increasing intensity in strength training and electrical muscle stimulation protocols; E. Henneman, G. Somjen, and D.O. Carpenter, "Functional Significance of Cell Size in Spinal Motoneurons," *Journal of Neurophysiology,* 28(3) (1965): 560-580.

Somehow, there was a belief going around that people would get hooked by the "only twenty minutes" slogan. I still see it every day on Instagram accounts. The problem is, if you understand and know about EMS training and all the details, yes, of course, twenty minutes is great compared to two hours in the gym. But with what we know today, it's not relatable or a hook for certain audiences. They simply don't relate to this point, and it's our job to give them a reference and hook them. More about this later.

But back to the facts. Some of us experienced the opposite in promoting "just twenty minutes." Prospects (the wrong ones) would debate how you could charge more than a regular gym membership or personal training while only providing twenty minutes of service. This is like comparing an apple with a pear — they look similar, but they are two completely different fruits.

I would promote EMS in magazines and newsletters; at BNI business breakfasts, open houses, and networking events; on social media (only Facebook at that time, 2010, and no ad campaigns, just posting on my personal page); and via affiliate marketing. I remember the first prices and packages introduced to me by the supplier and the first EMS training franchise. The concept was this: Train twenty minutes a month and pay the same fee as a big box gym — approximately $30. The target audience was young people who wanted to stay fit with minimal effort. Instead of going to a gym, they would go to an EMS studio once a month. Sorry, not sorry, but it's ridiculous. I don't have to tell you that training once a month, even with electro-muscle stimulation, is not enough.

We won't delve too deeply into EMS training philosophy here, but understanding training principles and the adaptability of the human body is crucial. Regardless of your target audience, they will struggle to see results and, therefore, find it challenging to become committed long-term members of your brand. Even training once a week for the price of a one-on-one session, which is still heavily promoted by some suppliers, does not challenge the body enough in the long term. You will see some improvements in the beginning but then quickly hit a plateau. And most of your clients won't be able to adapt their nutrition as quickly, so the outcome will be *no results*. No results lead to low retention rates, high churn rates (also known as attrition, or the rate at which clients leave your business), and no referrals. Not good.

The other big problem is the price point. EMS training studios follow the widespread but broken EMS studio model. This approach might work in the beginning when you are the manager and main trainer. However, any long-term concept where you hire good trainers makes this model unsustainable. Simply starting an EMS training business to remain self-employed cannot be the "big opportunity" that suppliers sell you on. I ran into this problem the moment I had more than one studio and couldn't work full-time as a trainer at my next location. The moment I had to hire a good supervisor or head trainer, the margins fell apart, and the business model no longer looked attractive at all.

This price point of approximately $30 per EMS training session then became a trend within the first market (Germany), and every new equipment owner who started out would copy these models and follow the supplier's suggestions.

That led to an immediate devaluation of the actual service, and new EMS training studio owners would barely think about their niche or their target market. At least I didn't. Still, out of my passion, excitement, and drive, I did it. With what I know today, I would definitely have started by defining my dream client avatar. But more about that in a bit.

COPYING BROKEN SYSTEMS

When I entered the world of EMS training, I was introduced to it mainly by the equipment supplier. They showed me other EMS training franchises and studios, but the problem was they all followed the same model. Let's call it the old marketing model. Over the past fifteen years, I have witnessed many people entering the EMS training world out of affection and passion for the health and fitness industry. Most individuals start this business because they see an opportunity to be part of a new movement that offers great potential. They believe they have a chance to build something big and fulfill their financial dreams. However, they quickly fall for the promises that suppliers sometimes make just to sell the equipment or make the process seem easy.

The truth is, in order to build a sustainable and successful EMS training business, you need more skills than just knowing how to operate the EMS equipment and provide a great training session.

FACING CHALLENGES

I want to clarify that I'm not trying to criticize EMS equipment suppliers, as their job is not to become full EMS business consultants and sales and marketing agencies. While they provide marketing tools like flyers and banners, templates for websites, and keywords for web searches, that may not be enough to build a fully equipped studio with high retention rates. To succeed, you need to understand how marketing works in your specific area and how marketing has recently evolved. More importantly, you need to know who you are serving and what results they desire. You need to identify where they gather and which influencers they follow, and create hooks to capture their attention and make them interested in what you have to offer.

However, understanding marketing and communication is not enough. In the EMS world, there are numerous hurdles to overcome when it comes to conversion. You need to know how to engage someone for the first time, get their interest, and convince them to show up for a trial session. This can be challenging because trying something new and going to a new location requires courage. You need exceptional skills to make it easy for them to take that step. Once they show up, you need to sell them on the idea of committing to you long-term and convince them that they won't regret it.

All of this is possible, but it requires a skill set that is often overlooked during the initial set-up phase for a new EMS business.

LESSONS LEARNED

I witness a lot of confusion, impatience, and frustration among EMS trainers and studio owners as they often have different expectations about the process. And they don't think it will take that much action every single day. But it does. Many think it will be easier than it is, requiring less daily effort, and assume they will receive more support from their suppliers. Just reading a simple guide on how to get the first one hundred clients is not enough. Relying entirely on a third-party digital marketing company often leads to frustration after high expectations, low studio capacities, and a lack of necessary skills to master the conversion game.

On top of that, you need the budget to hire an agency and run ads. Did you know that successful EMS studio franchises allocate $50K on ad spend in the pre-opening phase to reach a certain capacity threshold, like the first one hundred members? But that's not all.

Indeed, challenges arise when dealing with different types of leads, such as cold, warm, and hot leads. Understanding the differences between these leads and knowing how to effectively engage with each is crucial. For instance, if you hire an agency to generate leads through a Facebook campaign, and you reach out to those leads a week later, your chances of converting them into customers are significantly reduced. Therefore, being well-informed about the expectations and strategies for working with different types of leads is essential for success. Additionally, a digital marketing agency often doesn't teach you what they are doing or help you with front-end skills, like how to convert leads into prospects. It can take a cold lead fifteen touchpoints and the perfect call and messaging scripts to warm up. Yes, that's right. Do you get an idea of how expectations can go wrong here?

If you choose to handle lead generation yourself, it requires a great deal of patience and time to learn the necessary skills. Additionally, the exponential development of technology poses a challenge. Staying up-to-date is crucial to keep pace with the ever-changing landscape.

OUTDATED EMS TRAINING MARKETING METHODS AND NECESSARY INNOVATIONS

We need to change. It is not helpful to blame someone else or to complain about our low capacity and conversion rates. Let's be grown-ups and identify which current marketing methods are outdated, identify our shortcomings, and recognize the areas that need change.

OUTDATED MARKETING METHODS

Traditional Print Advertising:

Relies heavily on flyers, brochures, and newspaper ads.

Weaknesses: Limited reach and engagement, particularly with younger demographics.

NECESSARY INNOVATIONS

Targeted Paid Digital Advertising:

Use platforms like Facebook, Instagram, and Google Ads to reach specific demographics. Run paid campaigns with irresistible offers for at least six weeks, charged upfront.

Implement retargeting campaigns to convert interested visitors into clients.

OUTDATED MARKETING METHODS

Cold Calling:

Interruptive and often seen as intrusive.

Weaknesses: Low conversion rates and can negatively impact brand perception.

**Generic
Email Blasts:**

Sending the same email to your entire contact list.

Weakness: High chances of being marked as spam.

NECESSARY INNOVATIONS

Content Marketing:

Create valuable content like blog posts, videos, and infographics. Establish your studio as an authority and attract organic traffic. Promote free challenges that engage prospects.

Repeat every sixty to ninety days to maintain engagement.

**Personalized Email
and Text Marketing:**

Segment your email list and tailor messages to different client groups. Use automation to send relevant emails based on client behavior. Reactivate leads that haven't joined yet.

OUTDATED MARKETING METHODS

One-Size-Fits-All Promotions:

Offering the same discounts or promotions to all clients.

Downside: Fails to address individual client needs.

Over-Reliance on Word of Mouth:

Passive approach to gaining new clients.

Downsides: Inconsistent and difficult to scale.

NECESSARY INNOVATIONS

Interactive Social Media Engagement:

Post engaging content on social media regularly, and use stories, live sessions, and interactive polls to connect with your audience.

Referral Programs:

Encourage current clients to refer friends and family by offering incentives. Track referrals and reward both the referrer and the new client.

OUTDATED MARKETING METHODS

Static Website Content:

Outdated, non-interactive websites.

Downsides: Lack of engagement and poor user experience.

Ignoring Social Media:

Not maintaining an active presence on social media.

Downside: Missing out on opportunities to connect with a wider audience.

NECESSARY INNOVATIONS

Website, SEO, and Local Search Optimization:

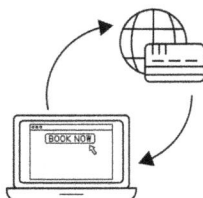

Optimize your website with an irresistible trial offer, easy booking, and search engine optimization. Focus on local SEO to attract clients in your area.

Client Testimonials and Case Studies:

Share success stories and testimonials on your website and social media. Showcase real results through before and after pictures within your EMS studio.

NECESSARY INNOVATIONS

Host Events:

Host open days and events to educate potential clients on the benefits of EMS training. Invite guest speakers and industry experts to provide extra value.

Collaborations and Partnerships:

Partner with local businesses, influencers, and health professionals. Cross-promote services to expand your reach. Start with trial sessions and build strong partnerships.

In chapter 6, I will dive deeper into these marketing innovations and more, giving you actionable steps to implement each strategy and how to transition from outdated methods to cutting-edge solutions that will transform your marketing efforts and fuel your growth.

DEVELOPING A NEW APPROACH

Developing a new business approach in the EMS training industry requires a shift in mindset, particularly in recognizing the importance of marketing and sales. It is essential to understand that customers will not simply walk into our studios and sign up without significant ongoing effort on our part.

To increase our chances of success, we must be willing to take daily actions. This includes implementing a proven success path. For example, conducting one hundred outreaches a day can help us reach potential customers consistently. Additionally, staying updated on marketing innovations and constantly working on improving our content, referrals, testimonials, case studies, and automations are crucial. I will explain this in detail in chapter 6.

In today's fast-paced world, it can be challenging to navigate the complexities of marketing. However, by embracing these strategies and utilizing effective automations and retargeting techniques, we can improve our chances of success.

TESTING AND REFINEMENT

The success of any EMS training business begins with the right attitude, mindset, and budget for sales and marketing. Both the business owners and trainers need to embrace the importance of these aspects and understand that they play a significant role in driving growth.

To achieve success, it's crucial to adopt a mindset of continuous improvement. This involves being open to testing new strategies, refining existing approaches, and constantly iterating on the success path. Through ceaseless experimentation, analysis, and optimization, we can identify what works best for our specific business and target audience.

It's also important to recognize that running an EMS training business is not just about having trainers and digital marketing. It requires viewing the business as one with various departments: operations, finance, customer service, and more. By acknowledging the multifaceted nature of the business and ensuring all departments are functioning effectively, we can create a solid foundation for growth and success.

WHY LONG-TERM MEMBERSHIPS ARE CRUCIAL FOR YOUR EMS BUSINESS SUCCESS

EMS trainers and studio owners often shy away from long-term memberships, opting instead for pay-as-you-go or month-to-month options to avoid handling customer objections. However, objections are a natural part of the sales process. When you lack sales training, it's easy to mistakenly believe that long-term memberships are the problem. In reality, it's your sales skills that need improvement. This book will teach you how to successfully sell long-term memberships, which is essential for several reasons:

Sustainable Transformation: People need to train long-term to achieve and maintain their new lifestyle. Quick fixes don't lead to lasting results.

Business Valuation: Your EMS business is evaluated based on your recurring revenue, not short-term packages.

Community Growth: Your EMS brand grows with a loyal community, which doesn't happen if customers view EMS as a quick fix and leave after a few sessions.

Sales Efficiency: Selling an eight-session pack repeatedly is harder and less efficient than securing long-term memberships.

Customer Retention: Long-term memberships improve customer retention, ensuring a steady stream of revenue and reducing the constant need for new customer acquisition.

Member Commitment: Long-term memberships foster a deeper commitment from clients, leading to better results and higher satisfaction.

Predictable Revenue: With long-term memberships, you have more predictable and stable revenue, allowing for better business planning and growth.

Enhanced Client Relationships: Building long-term relationships with clients enhances trust and loyalty, leading to more referrals and positive word-of-mouth.

Brand Loyalty: Clients who commit long-term are more likely to become advocates for your brand, helping to establish a strong reputation in the community.

Reduced Marketing Costs: With a stable base of long-term members, you can reduce marketing costs and focus more on member engagement and satisfaction. You can buy them more presents :).

Remember, the key to selling long-term memberships lies in improving your sales skills. This book will guide you through the process, equipping you with the knowledge and techniques needed to overcome objections and secure long-term commitments from your clients. Keep reading to transform your EMS business into a thriving, sustainable venture.

DATA-DRIVEN DECISION-MAKING

Using analytics and metrics to track performance is crucial. Understanding and analyzing data allows you to make informed and strategic decisions to improve your business. Here are some key points to consider:

Data provides valuable insights into the performance of your EMS studio. It helps you identify trends, measure the effectiveness of your marketing efforts, and understand customer behavior. By analyzing data, you can uncover opportunities for growth, identify areas of improvement, and make data-driven decisions.

Start by identifying the key metrics that are most relevant to your studio's success. These may include the total number of clients, active clients, client retention rate, leads generated, conversion rate, referral rate, revenue per client, and customer acquisition cost (CAC), among others. Tracking these metrics consistently will give you a clear picture of your studio's performance over time.

Regularly reviewing and analyzing your data will allow you to identify trends and patterns. For example, you can determine which marketing channels generate the most leads, which client segments are the most valuable, or which campaigns drive the highest conversion rates. Understanding these trends will help you allocate resources effectively and focus on strategies that have the biggest impact.

Analyzing data can provide insights into customer behavior and preferences. By understanding why clients exit your studio, you can make improvements to your services or address any issues. Additionally, tracking referral rates can help you identify clients who are more likely to refer others, allowing you to focus on nurturing those relationships.

Armed with data, you can make more informed decisions regarding your marketing strategies. For example, if you find that a particular marketing channel is not generating enough leads, you can reallocate your resources to more effective channels. By analyzing the data, you can identify opportunities for improvement and optimize your marketing efforts to maximize results.

Remember, tracking and analyzing data may seem challenging at first, but it is essential for the growth and success of your studio. By embracing data-driven decision-making and consistently monitoring your metrics, you can make strategic adjustments and capitalize on opportunities for improvement. Start today by looking at every single number in your business. Use that information to drive your marketing efforts and focus on areas that have the biggest leverage.

The Story of Marc F.

Marc F. is a personal trainer from Germany with over a decade of experience in the fitness and EMS fields. He worked as a PT while pursuing a bachelor's degree in economics and nurturing his passion for Olympic weightlifting. Marc trained hard every week, striving to excel in his sport.

But then, injuries began to plague him. First, it was his knees, then his back, and finally, his shoulder forced him to stop. No doctor could help him. Desperate for a solution, he researched various options and stumbled upon EMS training. Initially, he thought it was a scam. For someone who had spent countless hours training, the promise of results with only a twenty-minute session seemed unrealistic.

Despite his skepticism, Marc decided to give EMS training a try. To his amazement, he became pain-free for the first time in a very long while. This newfound relief motivated him to not only become a frequent user but also to spend three years working in an EMS training studio. After going to work for another EMS studio for one year, he was offered the opportunity to buy the studio and seized the chance to embark on a new journey of self-employment.

Looking back, Marc admits he was quite naïve when he started his first business. His expertise lay solely in training, and he had little knowledge of the business side, especially sales and marketing. He made numerous mistakes, such as not filing his taxes correctly, mismanaging bookkeeping, and neglecting sales and marketing. Just one-and-a-half years into owning the studio, the COVID-19 pandemic hit, presenting Marc with his first major crisis as an entrepreneur. In desperation, he sought help and found EMS Mastermind. Together, we systematically turned his business around to make it profitable and efficient.

The studio he bought was what we call a "broken system." Customers had no agreements, there were numerous side agreements with the previous owner, and the price structure barely allowed for profits. When challenged to change the business concept, Marc faced his biggest fears: upsetting his clients, losing customers, and facing rejection. But he trusted the process, and with baby steps, we transformed the studio into a personal EMS training brand with values reflected in every aspect of its operations. Marc defined his dream client and created the perfect irresistible offer for this niche. He built a new booking app, changed the billing cycle to every four weeks, and introduced weekly charges. He now offers only long-term memberships like twelve- and twenty-four month terms, alongside a high-ticket upfront offer, significantly increasing his cash flow and revenue.

Today, Marc allows himself to work only from Monday to Friday, taking weekends off. He has established terms and conditions, creating healthy boundaries that keep relationships with clients sustainable. Operations are streamlined, following a clear success path, and he is accountable for his sales and marketing actions weekly. His business is constantly growing, as is his confidence and the success of his clients. The best part? His biggest fear of losing old customers was unfounded — no one left. Marc now boasts one of the best retention rates I've ever seen in the industry. This year, Marc is getting married and is excited about building his family. The best is yet to come.

LOOKING TO THE FUTURE

Looking into the future, there are three important components that studio owners should focus on to ensure continuous improvement and success. Let's break them down:

1. **Keep Your Tech Up-to-Date**
    It's essential to stay current with the latest technology and not be afraid to learn and adopt new tools and platforms. By understanding and utilizing the advancements in technology, you can streamline your operations, enhance customer experience, and stay ahead of the competition.

2. **Evolve Your Marketing**
    The marketing landscape is constantly evolving, and it's important to embrace change and adapt to new trends and strategies. By staying ahead of the curve and being open to innovation, you can effectively reach your target audience, engage with them, and drive business growth.

3. **Join Your Community**
    In the early days of the EMS business industry, studio owners often viewed each other as competitors, leading

to a sense of isolation. However, now is the time to come together as like-minded entrepreneurs and build a strong community. By collaborating, sharing insights, and setting high standards, the industry as a whole can grow and succeed. Being part of an empowering community allows you to learn from industry peers, exchange best practices, and collectively elevate the industry to new heights.

By focusing on continuous learning, embracing change, and being part of an empowering community, studio owners can position themselves for long-term success and contribute to the growth and advancement of the EMS industry.

Join our community now:

CHAPTER 4

BROKEN SYSTEMS: THE FIVE THINGS YOU'RE GETTING WRONG

I was around nine months into operating my very first EMS training studio when I received a call from my mom. Her voice sounded anxious (she is always anxious, but she was literally freaking out) as she said, "Jemima, I saw an advertisement in today's newspaper. There's another person opening an EMS studio here in the city." At that moment, I felt her anxiousness triggering a physical reaction in me too. I felt butterflies in my stomach, my head started racing, and I tried to figure out what this really meant. All the while, my body was triggered by my mom's reaction as she perceived this news instantly as a threat.

It was definitely not the best news. I was already buried in work, operating every day of the week, trying to convert every potential prospect into a member. I signed up customer after customer, and although I was excited about my growing business and the success I was having with EMS training, the thought of competition stung.

The person my mom mentioned was well-known in the city, a personal trainer with years of experience and a solid reputation. I couldn't help but feel the weight of self-doubt creeping in. I wasn't a trainer before owning my EMS studio. I had jumped into this industry after discovering the power of EMS and quickly completed my certifications. It felt like a huge opportunity, and I was determined to make the most of it. But now, faced with this competition, I questioned myself: *Am I good enough? Will I lose customers? What is going to happen next?*

As I wrestled with the anxiety, I took a couple of deep breaths. I realized that the presence of another EMS studio could actually be a blessing. After pausing, and breathing, I was able to lead my thoughts in a positive direction, not based on fear but believing there was something positive in this. I wanted to pursue this with faith. Instead of diminishing my business, it brought credibility to the EMS concept in our city. I wasn't the only one doing something innovative with electro-muscle stimulation; now, there was another established figure doing the same thing. From time to time, I would hear the gossip of people who would call me "the lady who does something with electro shocks." LOL! Well, that would be over, I thought. This dual presence showcased the value of EMS training and hopefully created greater interest among potential clients.

More people doing EMS training. More marketing. More education. More interest. More business.

What I learned from this experience was profound: competition doesn't necessarily mean defeat. It can mean more opportunities.

Competition can enhance the industry as a whole. The fear I initially felt transformed into motivation, pushing me to refine my services and deepen my connection with my clients. I embraced the challenge and focused on what made my studio unique, all while fostering a sense of community within the EMS landscape. Of course, first, it triggered my fears and insecurities.

> Competition doesn't necessarily mean defeat. It can mean more opportunities.

In the end, I found my footing and grew stronger, turning what once felt like a setback into a stepping stone for success. And by the way, it would happen over and over again. My journey taught me that, almost always, challenges can lead to unexpected opportunities, and it's our response to those challenges that defines our path.

In this industry, we need to set the standards together. We need to help each other by not devaluing our prices and trying to be cheaper than our competitors. We need to know that we all help each other by promoting and educating the world about electro-muscle stimulation. But we need to stay strong when there is unfair competition. When competitors undercut our services, it's important to stick with our values. Often, they don't survive long. There will be situations that shake you and baffle you, but every day, you can choose faith over fear. Below are five common misconceptions or errors that may impede your progress in the EMS training industry.

THE FIVE BELIEFS I GOT WRONG IN MY EMS JOURNEY

In the first years of operating my EMS studios, I made several critical mistakes that shaped my journey. Here are the five things I got wrong:

1. **I Believed I Had to Figure It Out Alone**
   I thought I had to navigate this journey by myself. I viewed everyone else in the same field as a competitor, which made them feel like enemies. This mindset blocked me from connecting with others or asking for their help.

2. **I Thought Asking for Help Made Me Look Weak**
   I avoided asking for help because I believed it would expose my weaknesses. This flawed belief only isolated me further and hindered my growth.

3. **I Feared Boundaries Would Lead to Rejection**
   I was convinced setting boundaries would push others away, but I learned that boundaries are essential for healthy relationships and personal growth.

4. **I Worried That Others Would Steal from Me**
   I feared that if I shared my ideas or strategies, others in the industry would steal them. This fear stifled collaboration and creativity, which are vital for success.

5. **I Believed I Was Not Enough**
   I constantly battled the feeling that I wasn't enough — smart enough, skilled enough, or experienced enough. This

pervasive self-doubt held me back from pursuing opportunities and reaching my full potential. It also made me vulnerable to engaging with people who didn't have my best interests at heart. I found myself in partnerships and collaborations that began with the wrong motives, often with individuals who lacked experience in or understanding of my field.

One of the most important lessons I've learned is that while it's crucial to learn from others, who you choose to learn from is even more important. Drawing inspiration from the journeys of successful entrepreneurs who have overcome similar doubts and fears, especially those in your niche or who have achieved what you aspire to, can be transformative. Surrounding yourself with the right people, those who genuinely support and uplift you, is key to overcoming self-doubt and reaching your full potential.

At this point, you may be wondering:

"Am I qualified to do this?"

I wondered that same thing. The unfairest thing I can do to myself is compare myself to others. Whenever I do it, my imposter syndrome shows up. I start questioning myself: *Am I actually qualified enough? Do I have the right to be here?* The feeling of inadequacy often gets triggered in me whenever customers leave (churn). That's why it is so important to connect with others and not isolate myself in my career. I know that I am competent; there is so much evidence of it. But these negative thoughts can easily creep in.

The best solution for overcoming challenges and achieving success in running my EMS training studio is to embody fierce faith and take massive action. The qualifications you absolutely need include being a certified trainer and holding an EMS trainer certification. These certifications are crucial to ensure that you provide the safest training possible for our clients.

Our mental health is the cornerstone of our success. We live in a very challenging time when there are so many threats to our mental health. We can easily get overwhelmed by the information overload on the internet and through apps and social media platforms. We can spiral into a state where we lose our clarity and confidence and get distracted, which costs us our success. It's important to have a daily routine for mental clarity, regulation, and calmness to keep our focus on the main goal.

Whatever we manifest on the outside is a reflection of our inside. I want you to take an empowering action before moving to the next chapter. Take a moment and grab a journal. Start by relaxing your body. If you wish, close your eyes and take a couple of deep breaths. Notice your breath and feel your presence in the here and now. Think of your dream outcome with your EMS training business. What would a day look like when you're living out your dream? What would your thoughts look like? Write everything in one column on the right side.

Now, think about your current daily assumptions and beliefs. What comes to mind? What are some of the limiting beliefs you have? What are you most afraid of? Write those down in the column on the left side. Now, for every limiting belief on the left side, such as "Will people pay x for my service?" or "Will they stay long term?" create a new empowering statement. For example, "My service brings value to my customers, who are grateful to me and are happy to pay for it, as I provide them with the most valuable things: health and time."

Turning Doubts and Fears into Trust and Faith

DOUBT/FEARS	TRUST/FAITH
Limiting Beliefs	**Empowering Beliefs**
People can't afford EMS training long-term.	My dream client values and invests in their health.
I'm not good enough to run a successful EMS business.	I have the skills and support to thrive in the EMS industry.
There aren't enough clients interested in EMS.	The market is full of people seeking innovative fitness solutions.
EMS training is too niche to grow my business.	EMS is a growing trend, and I'm at the forefront of this industry.
I have to do everything myself to succeed.	Delegating and collaborating with experts accelerates my success.
It's too risky to invest in marketing.	Smart investments in marketing lead to consistent growth and high returns.
My competitors have more resources and experience.	I offer unique value that sets my EMS business apart from the competition.
I need to work harder, not smarter, to succeed.	Streamlining and automating processes will help me achieve more with less effort.
Clients won't commit to long-term EMS programs.	My clients are dedicated to their long-term health and fitness goals.
If I raise prices, I'll lose customers.	My services are worth every penny, and clients are willing to pay for quality.

Identifying fear-based behaviors means recognizing common patterns of behavior driven by fear, such as procrastination, perfectionism, and avoidance. How do those get triggered? In which situations do you fall into these patterns?

Let's address fear head-on. Know that there are more strategies for confronting and managing fear, including visualization, positive self-talk, and reframing negative thoughts. Let's give fear no room to expand in your mind. Let's move forward with trust and faith. Let's cultivate resilience by building the fortitude to handle negative challenges and setbacks with confidence and determination!

See you in the next chapter.

CHAPTER 5

THE FIRST STEP ON THE ROAD TO EMS BUSINESS SUCCESS IS KNOWING YOUR IDEAL CLIENT

I remember sitting at the kitchen table in my little basement apartment in Wuppertal, Germany, in 2009, thinking if I could only have ten clients, then I would be relieved. If I could at least cover my expenses, I could start living my dream as an EMS trainer, and I could do all day what I love. I couldn't sleep because I had just been introduced to EMS, and the excitement had my head racing. I had found the tool that would change the fitness industry forever. This inspired me to create my first EMS concept, which would later be trademarked as my30minutes. I still didn't know how to finance my first EMS machine, but my desire didn't let me rest. I knew I wanted it so badly, and I wouldn't stop until I had it. I would have taken anyone as a client in the first months of my operations, and I did... LOL. I just wanted to get started, put that suit on people, get going with my life-changing concept, and prove EMS really worked.

In my first year, I was too busy to even realize that I was training a lot of people who drained the life out of me and who I probably attracted because of my own unhealed trauma. They were people I didn't like, who would challenge me by overstepping my boundaries, not showing up to their appointments, complaining, or not paying. I have to say, not all of my new clients were like this, but when I clashed with these clients, there were moments when I asked myself, *Why am I doing this?* even though it was my dream come true.

Today, I know two things about finding your dream client: knowing who you actually want to work with saves energy, and once you do the due diligence work to find them, it creates an abundance you can't even grasp yet. If you are willing to put in the work, you will experience it. The best part is that you have the chance to attract people you actually like, people who will appreciate you and your service. People who you don't have to convince over price.

So, this chapter, which is your entry into the eight success steps, is more than worth it. And remember, you will spend a lot of time with your dream client! Sometimes more than with your friends and family. Create a vision of your dream client, also known as a dream client avatar, and they will appear in real life — just like you have appeared in mine, so I can help you reach your result faster and with happiness. No energy vampires.

Your background and experience play a significant role in determining your area of expertise and the type of customers you can effectively serve. For example, if you have a background in athletics or have been an athlete yourself, you may have a unique understanding of the needs and goals of athletes. On the other hand, if you are coming from a self-experienced pain point, like a mom who worked in corporate America and dealt with pain and is now helping other moms get fit and pain-free, you will have a different perspective and expertise.

It's important to acknowledge the uniqueness of each individual who enters the EMS training industry. Every person has their own goals, preferences, and challenges. By recognizing this, you can focus on identifying your niche and catering to their specific needs. As the saying goes, "The riches are in the niches." Instead of trying to serve all customer segments, it's more beneficial to specialize and become an expert in a particular niche. I see hooks every day like "EMS is for people with no time/back pain," and so on. First of all, nobody knows what EMS is, and in the worst case, they think it's emergency services. The best you can hope from posting this kind of hook on social media is it will attract other EMS studios — but not your dream client. Instead, say:

★ I work with/help women 40+ getting their pre-baby body back in no time!

★ I help aspiring female entrepreneurs build their dream bodies without burning out.

★ I work with corporate executives to regain their work-life balance and prioritize their health.

★ I help elite athletes optimize their performance and recovery with new EMS technology.

★ I assist women 60+ in staying active and strong so they can enjoy their life and grandkids to the fullest!

★ I help holistic wellness seekers incorporate EMS training into their routines for enhanced mind-body synergy.

★ I support new moms in rebuilding their core strength and confidence after childbirth without spending hours in the gym.

★ I help women struggling with stubborn weight to shed those extra pounds and feel amazing in their skin again.

★ I assist remote professionals in staying fit and energized, even when working long hours at home.

Surprisingly, the more specific and vivid you draw the portrait of your dream client, the more universal your dream client becomes. But the more generalized your description, the less your dream client will identify with it.

Trying to cater to everyone may dilute your expertise and effectiveness. By focusing on a specific segment and understanding their needs deeply, you can provide tailored solutions and guarantee results. This not only helps you stand out in the industry but also contributes to the overall growth and success of the EMS industry as a whole.

Take the time to reflect on your skills, expertise, and the type of customer you prefer to work with. Identify the segment where you shine the most and where you can truly make a difference. By focusing on your niche and delivering exceptional results, you can establish yourself as an expert in that area and attract customers who align with your values and goals.

ASSESS YOUR CURRENT CLIENT BASE

If you already operate an EMS studio, reflect on your past experiences. Review your existing customer data and interactions to glean insights into your current client base.

Identify your favorite standout clients who align closely with your ideal client profile based on characteristics, behaviors, and preferences.

Answer Key Questions

Gather demographic information such as age, gender, occupation, social circles, and location to paint a clearer picture of your target audience.

Explore psychographic factors, including interests, values, pain points, frustrations, fears, and motivations, to understand the deeper needs and desires of your ideal client.

Use Client Feedback and Testimonials

Collect and analyze client feedback, testimonials, and reviews to identify recurring themes, positive experiences, and areas for improvement to refine your ideal client profile.

Conduct Surveys and Interviews

Initiate conversations with existing clients through surveys, interviews, or informal discussions to gather first-hand insights.

Ask target questions about client preferences, goals, challenges, and perceptions to gain a deeper understanding and refine your ideal client persona.

Create Your Dream Client Avatar

Consolidate all this information into detailed client personas, including demographic and psychographic details, pain points, goals, and preferences.

Craft visual representations of your ideal client personas to provide a clear and tangible reference for future marketing and decision-making.

Take Action Today

Set a timeline and action plan for implementing the client identification process, starting with immediate steps to gather information and insights.

Recognize that client preferences and market dynamics may change over time, so commit to regular reviews and updates of your ideal client profile to ensure relevance and effectiveness.

USING AI

We have arrived in a century of artificial intelligence and rapidly advancing technology. I am not here to discuss the pros and cons of AI, but it's a tool worth mentioning as it can help you in your daily processes.

What Is a Chatbot?

A chatbot is an AI-powered tool that helps generate text based on the prompts you provide. (Some current examples include ChatGPT, Google Gemini, and Claude.) It's like having a personal assistant who can draft emails, create marketing content, answer questions, generate ideas, and much more. You can provide information (called a prompt) on nearly any topic, and it will assist with brainstorming, writing, or even technical queries. It's particularly useful for automating tasks, streamlining communication, and offering personalized advice.

Why Prompt Writing is Game-Changing

Writing the right prompts is key because it directs the AI tool to give you the exact results you need. The clearer and more specific your prompts, the better the outcome. Knowing how to ask the right questions can help you unlock the full potential of tools like ChatGPT, making complex tasks easier and faster to complete.

AI Prompt Example:

> *Act as an expert Instagram social media market-er specializing in health and wellness for women. Conduct detailed market research to identify and analyze the following for women aged 40+: Ten frustrations, ten desires, ten fears, and ten pain points. These women are busy working professionals, business owners, or career-driven individuals who also have families. They are mid to upper class, high-end, and highly focused on improving their fitness levels. They may experience physical challenges like back pain or perimenopause symptoms and work out purposefully, enjoying activities like tennis but disliking the visible effects of aging on their bodies. They are also interested in biohacking, longevity tools, and staying fit, strong, and toned as mothers. Organize the results in a structured table format with the x-axis labeled 1–10 and the y-axis labeled Frustrations, Desires, Fears, and Pain Points. Provide actionable insights, where applicable, to help in content creation and targeting for Instagram campaigns.*

Download our free dream client workbook here:

Creating Compelling and Relevant Marketing Materials That Resonate With Your Dream Client

Understanding the preferences and pain points of your dream client is crucial for successful marketing campaigns for several reasons:

1. Relevance. By understanding your target audience's preferences, you can create marketing campaigns that are relevant to their needs and interests. When your messaging resonates with your dream client, they are more likely to pay attention, engage with your content, and consider your offerings.

2. Personalization. Knowing your dream client's pain points allows you to personalize your marketing messages and offer solutions that directly address their specific challenges. This personalized approach makes your marketing efforts more effective and increases the chances of converting leads into customers.

3. Emotional Connection. By understanding your dream client's pain points, you can tap into their emotions and create a connection. When people feel understood and supported, they are more likely to trust your brand and develop a long-term relationship with your business.

4. Differentiation. Understanding your dream client's preferences helps you differentiate your brand from competitors. By highlighting the unique features and benefits that are most important to your audience, you can position your offerings as the best solution for their specific needs, giving you a competitive edge.

5. Cost Efficiency. Tailoring your marketing campaigns to your dream clients saves you time and resources. Instead of wasting resources on generic messaging that may not resonate with anyone, you can focus your efforts on the specific audience that is most likely to convert. This increases the efficiency of your marketing spend and maximizes your return on investment.

Understanding the preferences and pain points of your dream clients is crucial for successful marketing campaigns because it allows you to create relevant, personalized, and emotionally resonant messages that differentiate your brand and drive meaningful results.

CHAPTER 6

8 EMS STUDIO SUCCESS STEPS

1. Who Is Your Dream Client
2. Irresistible Offer
3. Master Conversion
4. Paid Leads
5. Organic Leads
6. Optimize All Channels
7. Master Retention
8. Systemize

Fig. 2. *8 EMS Studio Success Steps*

There are various reasons why an EMS studio might struggle to take off as envisioned. Recently, I received a message from a concerned client who shared that a colleague in the industry mentioned, "I'm one year in, I have seventy clients, and I'm not even breaking even." This revelation sparked a lot of concern, as it does for many who enter this industry with high hopes.

People venture into EMS for different reasons. Some have been introduced to the concept by a supplier and believe it's a great investment opportunity; others are driven by passion. Some come from a background in personal training or EMS training and are excited about opening their own studio, and others are introduced to the equipment and see the potential it offers. Yet, despite these diverse motivations, many studios struggle to gain traction right away.

Several factors can contribute to this challenge. They may not know who their dream client is, or perhaps their pricing strategy is misaligned with the market. Oftentimes, they replicate something they've seen elsewhere without considering if it truly fits their unique situation, which can lead to undervaluing their services.

Through my years of consulting with EMS studio owners, I've found that a significant part of the issue lies in managing an EMS studio, a lack of know-how, and unrealistic expectations. Many owners mistakenly believe that the EMS equipment sells itself. While it is indeed an incredible tool that initially captivates and inspires, the reality is that potential clients often don't know it exists or understand its benefits.

If studio owners lack sufficient business and marketing knowledge, are not up-to-date with current trends, or have unrealistic expectations about lead generation budgets and the time required to convert leads, they can quickly become overwhelmed. Marketing is not a one-time effort; it requires consistent, daily action.

With all the work I have done over the years and from my own experiences as a studio owner facing similar challenges, I developed a clear, straightforward, eight-step path. This approach not only leads to tangible results but also helps identify the weakest areas within the EMS business. By strengthening these areas, we can take the necessary actions to elevate the studio's capacity, ensuring it not only breaks even but establishes a solid proof of concept — making real profits in the process.

Now we will explore how to navigate these challenges effectively, setting you on a path toward success on your EMS journey. Let's dive in and discover how to unlock the full potential of your studio!

SETTING THE RIGHT EXPECTATIONS

Your own mindset, attitude, and work ethic play the biggest role in whether the roadmap will lead you to success. Building a successful EMS training business is not luck; it's hard work and dedication.

Sales and marketing are the most important components in a business. Without them, there is no business. Have you accepted that this will be a big part of your operation? Have you set aside time and investment to grow this? Are you ready to do this work every day? Because that's what it takes: daily repetition of sales and marketing actions. I am not sugarcoating here 'cause that won't get you anywhere close to where you want to be. It's going to be challenging at first, but it gets easier. And remember, all great things are hard at first.

You can't skip a step. Here is the roadmap to your success:

STEP 1: Identify Your Dream Client

Thanks to your work in the previous chapter, you've already completed Step 1. Congratulations!

STEP 2: Create Your Premium Offer

The next important step is crafting an offer that is so attractive, so unmatched, so unbeatable that your dream EMS client can't wait to buy it from you and start your service. As Jeffrey Gitomer says, "People don't like to be sold — but they love to buy."[6] And I like to add that they love to buy, *especially* if they feel they get a bargain.

---

6 Jeffrey Gitomer, "People Don't Like to Be Sold, but They Love to Buy," https://www.gitomer.com/people-dont-like-to-be-sold-but-they-love-to-buy/.

They love to get more value than they pay for. And that is exactly what we are doing when we develop unique, value-driven offers and packages that address the specific needs and desires of your dream EMS client. We go through this step in depth in chapter 8.

STEP 3: Master Conversion Techniques

Every lead that comes through needs nurturing. How, when, and what you reply to the lead are crucial if you are to convert them into a new EMS studio member.

How: Always reply with empathy, excitement, and understanding, addressing specific concerns while highlighting the benefits of EMS.

When: Respond promptly, ideally immediately or within a few hours, to keep the lead warm and engaged.

What: Tailor your replies to the lead's specific situation, reinforcing the value of EMS training and offering solutions to their concerns.

The following are the nurturing phases you have to master:

1. Getting them booked (first connection)
2. Getting them to show up

3. Getting them to sign up
4. Getting them to bring you referrals
5. Getting them to stay

Ever wished you had the perfect responses to your prospects' most common concerns and questions all in one place?

I've developed a master conversion document that includes the most common questions prospects ask and objections they pose, along with efficient and impactful responses you can give to close the deal more confidently.

This guide is your cheat sheet for handling client conversations like a pro. You will find it at the end of this book in appendix A.

This could be the game changer you've been waiting for!

STEP 4: Learn to Generate Organic Traffic

Build a comprehensive organic marketing strategy to increase visibility and attract potential clients to your EMS training studio. Use the following strategies to drive organic traffic to your website and physical location:

Content Marketing
- Create valuable content like blog posts, videos, and infographics and share them on social media (currently,

Instagram seems to be the place to attract most dream EMS customers).

- Provide value daily through content to your dream EMS client (again, focus on Instagram).
- Establish your studio as an authority in EMS training and attract organic traffic.

Social Media Engagement

- When people opt in, follow you, or like your posts, be proactive and reach out to them — don't wait for them to approach you.
- Take consistent daily action — we recommend one hundred outreaches a day (use our warm lead script in appendix C).
- Use stories, live sessions, and interactive polls to connect with your audience.
- Run a free x-week transformation challenge every sixty to ninety days that attracts prospects to opt in and engage with you.
- Announce the winner and reach out to the rest with our warm lead script (see appendix C) — repeat every sixty to ninety days.

Personalized Email and Text Marketing

- Segment your email list and tailor messages to different client groups.
- Use automation to send timely, relevant emails based on client behavior.
- Reactivate leads who haven't joined yet.

Referral Programs:
- Encourage current clients to refer friends and family by offering incentives.
- Track referrals and reward both the referrer and the new client. For example:
  o Pay the referrer US$100 in cash and put them on a visible board in your studio to celebrate them.
  o Give the new customer a special bonus that adds value.

Client Testimonials and Case Studies
- Share success stories and testimonials on your website and social media.
- Hang before and after pictures within your EMS studio (the best place is where the sales conversation happens).
- Build credibility and trust by showcasing real results.

Collaborations and Partnerships:
- Partner with local businesses, influencers, and health professionals.
- Cross-promote services and expand your reach within the community.
- Always start with a trial session experience when approaching these collaborations and partnerships.
- Win them over from the start to make them your biggest fans and promoters for EMS.
- When they commit themselves to EMS training and get results, these partnerships will work out great.

When you combine our warm lead script (see appendix C) with these tactics, you can attract organic traffic, draw more visitors to your website, studio, and landing pages, and increase your trial sessions.

STEP 5: Get More Leads With Paid Traffic Acquisition

Master the art of using targeted paid advertising campaigns to strategically promote your offers and services on platforms like Facebook, Instagram, and Google Ads to connect directly with your dream clients and drive highly qualified leads to your funnel, social media accounts, and website. Run paid campaigns for at least six weeks with an irresistible offer that you can charge for upfront. This will help you finance your marketing efforts.

Because paid traffic acquisition is incredibly complex and requires a deep understanding of targeting, optimization, and analytics, many entrepreneurs find it invaluable to collaborate with experienced experts or agencies (like EMS Mastery) to achieve the best results.

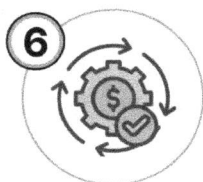

STEP 6: Optimize all Channels

Optimize your website with an irresistible trial offer that is easy to book and will optimize search engines to increase visibility. Focus on local SEO to attract clients in your area. Continuously monitor and analyze the performance of your organic and paid traffic channels to identify areas for improvement and optimization. Adjust your marketing strategies, messaging, and targeting based on data-driven insights to maximize the effectiveness of each traffic source.

STEP 7: Master Client Retention

The 5 Pillars of Retention

1. **Comprehensive Education on EMS and Effective Outreach Strategies**
   Educate clients thoroughly on the benefits of and science behind EMS. Provide them with knowledge that empowers them to see value in their sessions.

Implement effective outreach strategies, such as informative emails, social media content, and workshops, to keep clients engaged and informed.

2. **Precise Attendance Tracking Methods for Monitoring Progress**

Implement an easy-to-use online booking system with convenient payment options to enhance the client experience. (Remember: When clients are in a long-term commitment, charge them every four weeks, not monthly, as some months have five weeks and service is always provided on a weekly basis. Otherwise, you are losing money.)

Use the system's attendance tracking feature to monitor client participation and progress. This data helps identify patterns and allows you to intervene if a client's attendance drops.

Regularly review this data to offer personalized encouragement or adjustments to their training program, ensuring they stay motivated and committed.

3. **Personalized Handwritten Cards for Building Stronger Connections**

Send personalized, handwritten cards to clients on special occasions like birthdays, anniversaries, or after achieving milestones. This gesture strengthens the personal connection between the client and your brand.

Acknowledge their progress and express genuine appreciation for their commitment, fostering loyalty and trust.

4. **Engaging Events to Foster Community and Client Engagement**

Organize regular events such as client appreciation days, fitness challenges, or educational seminars about the benefits of EMS training. Use these events to demonstrate your expertise and attract new clients.

Invite guest speakers, doctors, practitioners, and industry experts to provide more value for guests by discussing topics that address the pain and desires of your dream client. These events provide opportunities for clients to connect with each other and the brand, creating a sense of community.

Encourage clients to bring friends or family members to these events, potentially converting them into new clients.

5. **Insightful Exit Interviews to Continuously Improve Your Services**

Conduct exit interviews with clients who decide to leave your program. Gather honest feedback on their experiences — what they liked, and what could be improved.

Use this feedback to make necessary adjustments to your services, ensuring continuous improvement and addressing any issues that could lead to future client retention challenges.

STEP 8: Systemize and Optimize

Develop a systematic approach to client acquisition that integrates all workflows and elements of the framework, from defining your dream EMS client to mastering retention. Document and automate key processes through your own CRM (or our EMM) platform, track performance metrics, and continuously refine your acquisition system to drive sustainable growth and success for your EMS training studio.

Do you want to learn more about these steps and how you can start implementing them for your EMS studio right now? Then scan the QR code:

Scan me!

CHAPTER 7

HOW TO OVERCOME NEGATIVE BELIEFS ABOUT SALES AND MARKETING

I remember the frustration when I ran my first Facebook campaign. I didn't know much about social media ads; I just wanted new customers, and I wanted them fast. When I started my first EMS studio, I didn't have to think about campaigns. My referral system worked so well that I had enough leads on a weekly basis to convert into clients. My sign-up rate was great. I was so excited, so convincing, and so confident that it was contagious to my prospects.

Once, a front desk manager observed me in the sales process. After the new client left, she said to me, "Jemima, even someone who doesn't want or hasn't planned on signing up has no chance of resisting you." What I can say is that I know it's the excitement, confidence, and empathy for the client that works for me.

However, this story isn't about my sales skills. It's about the fact that this alone didn't help me when trying to generate more leads. At this point, I not only had to support myself but also my new trainers. And they were in a completely different situation than me. Most of them lacked excitement, confidence, and overall sales and lead-nurturing skills.

I would go out to a social gathering and have three trial sessions booked for the next week. But my paid trainers wouldn't go out with the intention of working leads while they were socializing. So, I had to come up with a system that would automatically generate leads for my studios and for my trainers. If I had known back then how hard this would be... Uff. My biggest problem was that I wasn't informed enough about the different streams of traffic — how they work, how long they take, how to access them, and what expectations to have. And I was too busy to take the time to pay attention and learn properly, or to even reflect on my own lack of patience and trust at that moment.

So, I just hired an agency. I actually hired multiple people and agencies. And what I learned was that I was in the way. First, I didn't know what they were doing, which led to bad choices with agencies that didn't have my best interests in mind, and I didn't learn back then what all this entailed. Today, I know what realistic numbers and budgets look like when running a campaign to get cold leads, how long it takes to get warm leads, and that most people — most trainers — will not ask for referrals out of fear of rejection, and the last thing they'll do is ask consistently.

What I've learned in the last fifteen years is that our beliefs and doubts are our worst enemies. Wrong expectations keep us in a small-minded mindset. Within this mindset, we limit ourselves, refuse to take responsibility and the next right step, and can fall into a cycle where we blame others. But worse, we hurt ourselves. We keep ourselves stuck and hinder progress while staying small.

Here are some of the most common and hindering negative beliefs and their impacts.

NEGATIVE BELIEFS ABOUT SALES AND MARKETING

Belief: "I will get many paying customers with a very small budget."

Truth: Effective paid campaign marketing often requires a reasonable budget to reach and engage potential clients effectively.

Belief: "I don't have money for marketing."

Truth: There are cost-effective marketing strategies that can yield significant results without a large financial commitment.

Belief: "I can't sell. Selling is unethical."

Truth: Selling is a valuable skill that helps people discover solutions that can improve their lives with EMS training.

Belief: "Sales and marketing are not important in an EMS training business."

Truth: Sales and marketing are essential components that drive growth and success in your EMS business.

Belief: "If I don't get immediate results, the campaigns are not working, and I should stop."

Truth: Successful marketing requires time, testing, and adjustment; persistence is key to achieving long-term results.

Belief: "I can't contact that person more than three times. That seems unprofessional."

Truth: Following up is a normal and necessary part of the sales process that shows dedication to helping potential clients.

Belief: "I am not good at this. This won't work for me."

Impact: These beliefs can prevent you from learning the reality about sales and marketing and hold you back from learning the most essential skills needed in order to succeed in this business. There is no magic Facebook campaign and marketing strategy. It takes budget, patience, persistence, and learning to nurture a lead.

Truth: With practice and the right strategies, anyone can improve their sales and marketing skills.

Fear of Market Saturation

Belief: "There are already too many EMS studios in my area. I won't be able to compete."

Impact: This belief can prevent you from confidently marketing your specific know-how and expertise to your dream customer and creating a niche that hasn't been developed yet.

Truth: Every EMS business has its unique strengths; you can carve out your niche by highlighting what sets you apart.

Doubt in the Technology

Belief: "Clients won't believe in the effectiveness of EMS compared to traditional training."

Impact: You and your team may struggle with effectively communicating the benefits of EMS, leading to lower client acquisition and retention. How often do you talk about it? How often do you train yourself?

Truth: Educating clients about the science and benefits of EMS can foster belief and trust in the technology.

Concern Over Client Retention

Belief: "Clients will only see EMS as a temporary solution and won't stick around long-term."

Impact: This can result in a lack of focus on building long-term relationships, memberships, and loyalty programs. Go to the premium offer and create your long-term program now!

Truth: By creating engaging EMS training programs and building strong relationships, clients can be encouraged to see EMS as a long-term fitness solution.

Worry About High Startup Costs

Belief: "The initial investment is too high, and I'm not sure I'll see a return quickly enough."

Impact: This belief may lead you to hesitate to start or expand your EMS business, as well as to be reluctant to invest in marketing or equipment upgrades.

Truth: When approached strategically, investing in your EMS business can lead to significant returns.

Self-Doubt in Business Acumen

Belief: "I'm great at training, but I'm not a good businessperson."

Impact: You may avoid crucial aspects of business management, such as financial planning, marketing strategies, or staff development. All you need to know is in chapter 11. Keep reading.

Truth: Business skills can be developed through education and experience, just like any other skill.

Fear of Competition From Traditional Gyms

Belief: "Traditional gyms and fitness studios offer more variety, and I can't compete with that."

Impact: This can lead to a lack of confidence in the uniqueness and value of EMS, resulting in weaker marketing and sales efforts.

Truth: EMS training offers unique benefits that can attract clients looking for efficient and effective workout solutions.

Doubt in Profitability

Belief: "EMS training is a niche market and won't be profitable enough to sustain my business."

Impact: This can't be further from the truth. As the riches are in the niches, this belief can prevent you from defining

your dream client, scaling your operations, or investing in growth opportunities.

Truth: EMS niche markets can be incredibly profitable when
approached with a strong marketing strategy and a
clear understanding of client needs.

Uncertainty About Client Demand

Belief: "There isn't enough demand for EMS training in
my area."

Impact: This belief can limit marketing efforts and discourage
you from fully exploring your target market.

Truth: Conducting market research can reveal untapped
demand and help you tailor your offerings to meet
local needs.

Fear of Negative Perception

Belief: "People might think EMS is just a fad or gimmick."

Impact: This can lead you to conservative marketing strategies and a lack of enthusiasm when you are promoting
the benefits of EMS training.

Truth: Educating the public about the proven benefits of EMS
training can change perceptions and build credibility.

Concern Over Rapid Technological Advancements

Belief: "Technology changes so quickly. What if my EMS
equipment becomes obsolete?"

Impact: This can cause hesitation to invest in new equipment or upgrade existing systems, hindering the ability to offer the latest and best services to clients.

Truth: Staying informed about EMS industry advancements can help you make strategic upgrades at the right time.

Fear of Not Meeting Client Expectations

Belief: "What if clients don't see the results they expect from EMS training?"

Impact: This can create anxiety about client satisfaction and lead to overly cautious training programs or under-promising results.

Truth: Setting realistic expectations and focusing on education can help clients understand their journey and progress. Instead of over-promising in the sales process, over-educate your clients about EMS training and be realistic about how long transformation really takes. Nothing under twelve months!

LIMITING BELIEF ABOUT PERSONAL TIME MANAGEMENT

Belief: "Running an EMS business will take up all my time, and I won't have work-life balance."

Impact: This can lead to burnout and prevent you from fully engaging in growing your business.

Truth: Implementing effective time management strategies and setting boundaries can lead to a successful business while maintaining a healthy work-life balance.

Don't feed your doubt; feed the big vision. I've created this framework to remind you of what's most important on this journey: your mindset.

6 STEPS TO SUCCESS

MINDSET

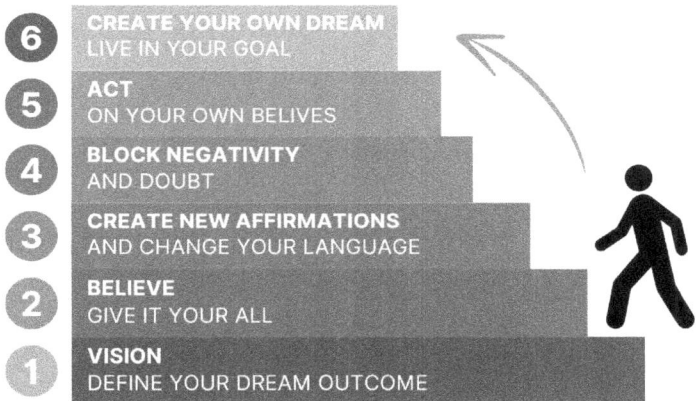

6 CREATE YOUR OWN DREAM
LIVE IN YOUR GOAL

5 ACT
ON YOUR OWN BELIVES

4 BLOCK NEGATIVITY
AND DOUBT

3 CREATE NEW AFFIRMATIONS
AND CHANGE YOUR LANGUAGE

2 BELIEVE
GIVE IT YOUR ALL

1 VISION
DEFINE YOUR DREAM OUTCOME

Fig. 3. 6 Steps to Success Mindset

SEEK SUPPORT AND GUIDANCE

My most hindering belief was that I had to figure everything out by myself. My lack of trust in people and my self-sufficiency were my worst enemies. Yes, there's always a risk component when entering into new business relationships, but if I learned one thing from my past and early years in the EMS business, it's that you are not meant to do it alone. You gain speed by learning from people who have been where you are right now. The important part is filtering out who works best for you and who is trustworthy.

It's also about accepting that you're not good at everything or that there are areas in the business where you're weak — not because *you are* weak, but because you lack knowledge. You can either try to learn the skill yourself or fast-track the process. But realistically, you can't run all departments yourself. Which departments are you strong in? Which can you outsource? Which can you delegate? Which can you automate? Where can you seek help?

Tap into support networks, mentors, and industry experts for guidance, advice, and encouragement in navigating challenges and overcoming doubts. Engaging with peers and fellow entrepreneurs in the EMS industry to share experiences, insights, and best practices for collective growth and success will be a game changer.

Scan here to join our free community chat:

CHAPTER 8

THE PERFECT OFFER

CREATE A PREMIUM EMS TRAINING OFFER

I remember the anxiety that hit me whenever I saw another EMS competitor advertising crazy discounts and ridiculous prices. Most of the time, they had just opened and were already flaunting a rock-bottom price. For a moment, I would panic, questioning my own pricing and offers. But here's the truth: No EMS studio can create life-changing results and sustain their business while selling themselves short.

Nothing is more unattractive than a business opportunity that isn't profitable and doesn't create life-changing results for its customers. What we really need is to create abundance — a high-ticket, premium EMS offer that can't be ignored. Let me walk you through how.

EMS Trial Session for Prospects

This is your chance to wow them from the start. It's not just a session; it's their first step into your world. Make it count by showing them the value behind electro-muscle stimulation and your service, and why your EMS training is different. Remember: A prospect likely doesn't know anything about EMS and has no clue what will happen in your EMS trial session, so maybe compare it to going to a normal gym, where they might tour the facility and then meet the sales manager. But in our case, it's totally different, and that's why it's important to explain to the prospect what they will be getting when they come to you.

Your Personal EMS Trial Session – Get Ready for a Transformative Experience!

Dear [Customer's Name],

We're thrilled to have you booked in for your upcoming **EMS trial session**! Here's a glimpse of what you can expect during your personalized consultation and workout session:

Customized 20-min EMS session – Value: $150

- **5 Minutes:** We'll begin with an introduction to the EMS program, where we familiarize you with the current and teach you how to pre-tense, breathe, and hold the basic position.
- **10 Minutes:** Experience a dynamic EMS session tailored specifically to your needs, combining the best of personal training with the power of electro-muscle stimulation.

- **5 Minutes:** Relax and unwind with recovery time, giving you a chance to reflect on the session and how EMS can transform your fitness journey.

In addition to your EMS session, you'll also receive a body composition scan and analysis (value $80), a comprehensive health and fitness consultation (value $80), and a basic nutrition evaluation (value $50) to help you understand your body's unique needs and maximize your fitness potential. Refreshments and the special undergarment (value $XX) will be provided as well.

Why You'll Love It: Our trial session is much more than just a workout. It's a personalized training experience where you'll see the true value of EMS technology and its ability to help you reach your fitness goals faster, whether you're looking to tone up, build strength, or improve your overall well-being. Clients in [Your City] are raving about the incredible results they achieve with EMS!

Exclusive Offer: This complete EMS experience worth $400 is just $40! Should you choose to continue with one of our packages or join our popular six-week challenge, the consultation and trial session will be completely free of charge.

However, if you decide not to proceed, a $40 consultation fee will apply.

We're confident you'll love your EMS session and the personalized attention you'll receive. If you have any questions or need more details before your trial, feel free to get in touch.

Looking forward to helping you unlock your fitness potential!

Sincerely,
[Your Name]

You can use this template for an email or phone call before and after booking. Educating the customer upfront is key. This is your pitch. Feel free to tweak it so it is perfectly unique to your EMS trial offer.

Set Up an EMS Challenge (Flexible, Short-Term)

Follow up the trial with a short-term challenge that delivers results. It's all about building their trust and showing them real, tangible progress.

Example: 6-Week Transformation Challenge:

- 12 x customized 20-min EMS sessions (value: $1,800)
- 2 x body composition analysis (value: $80)
- basic nutritional guidance (value: $50)
- undergarment and towel rental (value: $90)

Total Value: $2,020

Limited Time Offer: $997

It is important to schedule clients that bought the six-week challenge immediately for a progress consultation after three weeks, to ensure they see the difference EMS training makes in their lives and seize the opportunity to upsell them. What you want to avoid is an end date in their mind. You want them to learn that this is their new lifestyle routine. In a progress consultation, you measure and scale them again, followed by the long-term offer introduction.

Pro Tip: When they commit to the twelve-month membership, you credit the remaining cost of the six-week challenge to the new membership payment.

Example: Remaining value of the six-week challenge after three weeks: $498.50. Price of new membership for two sessions a week: $499. So they have already paid for the first months.

Offer a Premium EMS Membership

This is where they lock in for the long term. Stack your offer with value that's impossible to resist.

Example: Premium 12-Month EMS Membership (two sessions a week)

- 8 x customized 20-min EMS sessions (value: $1,200)
- Monthly body composition analysis (value: $80)
- Ongoing nutritional guidance (value: $50)
- Accountability group (value: priceless)
- Quarterly events with health experts (value: $120)
- Free refreshments, towels, and undergarments

Total value? Up to $1,490. But with a limited-time price of $499 every four weeks, your offer becomes absolutely irresistible. And to sweeten the deal, give them an upfront payment option where they save even more. Watch as the fear of missing out (FOMO) kicks in!

Offering an upfront payment option gives you the chance to collect larger amounts of cash each month, which boosts your cash flow and strengthens client commitment. It's a game changer.

Even if you're not ready to sell high-ticket packages, put them on your price list anyway. Trust me, more people are willing to pay upfront than you think. Not only do they save, for example, an extra 20%, but they also avoid inflation (roughly 15% per year). So, if they have the funds available, they're getting the best deal possible. That's when it makes sense to offer sessions for as low as $50.

Stack Your Premium EMS Offer

Now, this is where the magic happens. Take everything you do for your dream client and list it out. Put a price tag on each service, and watch as the value of your offer increases.

Don't have all those services in place just yet? Don't stress. Start with what you have and build from there. Remember, the goal is to show your clients that this is no ordinary EMS fitness program. This is their solution.

Use Scarcity

Scarcity works — period. Let them know that you only have limited spots in your EMS training program. Your time is the most valuable thing you can offer, and it's not endless. The sooner they sign up, the better.

Create Urgency

Your offer won't last forever. Make it clear that they need to act now. Whether it's available for twenty-four hours or just until the end of the day, they need to feel the pressure to commit.

Add a Risk-Free Guarantee

Your goal is to create results, not just to collect a check. Show them that you're confident enough in your service to offer a risk-free guarantee. And explain what they need to do on their end — show up to their sessions and follow your advice — so they know they're part of the success equation too. Check appendix B for the sample money-back guarantee.

Use Bonuses as the Final Push

Who doesn't love a bonus? Think of something special you can throw in right before they sign on the dotted line — whether it's a free undergarment kit, a weight loss starter pack, or a VIP coaching session. Use it to push them over the edge right when they're hesitating.

Follow these steps, and trust me, no competitor will be able to touch you. And when your dream clients start feeling that FOMO, they won't be able to say no.

SARAH'S STORY: FROM DOUBT TO SUCCESS

Sarah had always been passionate about fitness. She opened her EMS studio with high hopes, knowing that her training expertise would help clients achieve their goals faster than traditional methods. But as weeks turned into months, Sarah noticed her studio wasn't as busy as she had anticipated. She was caught up in the daily grind — providing EMS sessions, managing operations, and handling customer service. It felt like there was no time for anything else. The idea of investing in marketing felt overwhelming, and to make things worse, she didn't see how spending her time and money on it would make a difference.

One day, Sarah confided in Lisa, a fellow EMS studio owner, who asked a simple question: "If you don't market your studio, how will new clients find you?" Sarah paused. The truth was, she relied mostly on word-of-mouth, but it wasn't enough.

Lisa explained how she had felt the same way in the beginning — overwhelmed and doubtful. She shared how things changed for her after learning about different marketing tools. "It's true, marketing doesn't always bring instant results, but the long-term growth is undeniable," Lisa said. She introduced Sarah to simple tools: social media, local partnerships, email campaigns, and targeted ads. Lisa also explained that understanding these tools and trusting the process were key. It wasn't about doing everything at once, but about being consistent and strategic.

Sarah took the leap. She started with a social media presence, posting educational content about EMS and sharing client success stories. She followed it up with a referral program and an email newsletter. The first few weeks were quiet, but gradually, inquiries started to come in. It wasn't overnight, but the growth was steady.

Months later, Sarah looked around her studio and saw how full her schedule was becoming. She no longer questioned the value of marketing; she embraced it. The learning curve had been steep, but the results spoke for themselves. Her studio was thriving, not just because of her great EMS sessions, but because she had taken the time to invest in marketing.

Sarah's success story spread among other EMS owners who, like her, had initially been skeptical of marketing. She became a source of inspiration for those who were once hesitant, proving that when you combine passion with smart marketing strategies, success is only a matter of time.

Sarah's Next Challenge: Mastering Time and Priorities

As Sarah's studio began to grow, she realized that marketing wasn't a one-time effort — it was an ongoing process. But balancing marketing with her daily responsibilities of running the studio, managing staff, and providing client sessions seemed overwhelming. Sarah knew that if she didn't find a way to integrate marketing into her already busy schedule, she could easily fall behind.

One evening, Sarah sat down and took a hard look at her week. She mapped out her commitments: client sessions, meetings, studio management tasks, and personal time. The picture was clear — her time was limited. However, instead of feeling defeated, Sarah decided to be strategic. She asked herself two key questions: What marketing activities will give me the highest return on investment? And how can I fit them into my schedule without sacrificing the quality of my client sessions or burning out?

Identifying Key Marketing Priorities

Sarah knew she couldn't do everything at once, so she focused on the activities that would move the needle the most.

Offline Marketing Efforts

Sarah organized quarterly events, such as open days, where she invited her customers to bring friends and family. To make these events appealing, she included guest speakers who added value. The first event was a significant learning experience, but Sarah was committed to improving and continued hosting these events, leading to increasing success over time.

She also attended local networking events, where she shared her passion and mission. This approach allowed her to build relationships and actively exchange referrals.

Creating Valuable Content

Sarah decided to create content that spoke directly to the needs and interests of her dream customers. She blocked out two hours each week to plan and create social media posts and blog articles that highlighted the benefits of EMS training, shared client success stories, and provided fitness tips. This content didn't just promote her business; it provided value and education, building trust with her audience.

Daily Lead Nurturing

Every day, Sarah dedicated a small window of time — thirty minutes in the morning and thirty minutes in the afternoon — to nurture her leads. Whether it was responding to inquiries, following up with potential clients, or sending out personalized emails to keep her leads engaged, she made sure that this task became a daily habit. By staying connected and nurturing those relationships, Sarah found that more leads were converting into paying clients.

Mastering Time Management

Sarah knew that consistency was key, but with so many responsibilities, she had to be smart about how she managed her time. She implemented a few strategies to ensure that marketing didn't fall by the wayside.

Instead of trying to create content daily, Sarah started batching her work. She would set aside time on Mondays to draft and schedule her social media posts and blog posts for the week. This way, marketing didn't feel like a daily chore, and she could focus on her clients the rest of the week.

Sarah realized that while she loved connecting with leads, she didn't need to do everything herself. She trained one of her team members to help with social media engagement and lead follow-ups, freeing up more of her time for high-priority tasks.

Sarah also learned to set clear, measurable goals for her marketing. Instead of vague objectives like "get more clients," she defined specific targets like "generate fifty new leads per month" or "post three pieces of content per week." This focus kept her efforts aligned with her broader business goals and made it easier to track her progress.

Results Through Focused Effort

After months of disciplined time management and focusing on key activities, Sarah's marketing efforts began to pay off in a big way. Her content resonated with her dream customers, and she noticed an increase in engagement on social media and her website. Most importantly, her lead nurturing efforts were converting more prospects into loyal clients.

Sarah's journey wasn't just about implementing marketing strategies; it was about learning how to balance them with her existing responsibilities and making the most of the time she had. She found that by focusing on the activities that aligned with her goals and using time management techniques, she could continue growing her business without sacrificing her sanity.

UNDERSTANDING ROI IN EMS MARKETING

Return on investment (ROI) is a critical metric used to evaluate the success of marketing efforts by measuring the profitability of an investment relative to its cost. It is calculated by comparing the revenue generated from marketing campaigns to the initial investment. A positive ROI indicates that the marketing initiatives are effective, yielding more revenue than the amount spent. Understanding ROI allows businesses to assess which strategies are driving results, optimize future marketing efforts, and make informed decisions about where to allocate resources for maximum impact.

MEASURE ROI: CALCULATE THE REVENUE IMPACT

Determine how many clients you need to meet your revenue goal.

Revenue Goal for 100% ROI: $4,000

(100% ROI on $2,000 investment)

Available Packages:

- **1 Session/Week:** $3,120 per year
- **2 Sessions/Week:** $5,200 per year
- **6-Week Transformation Challenge:** $997

Conversions Needed to Achieve $4,000:

1. **One new client for the 2 Sessions/Week package:**
   - $5,200 (exceeds $4,000 goal)
2. **Two new clients for the 1 Session/Week package:**
   - $3,120 x 2 = $6,240 (exceeds $4,000 goal)

3. **Four new clients for the 6-Week Transformation Challenge package:**
   - $997 x 4 = $3,988 (almost meets $4,000 goal)

4. **Combination of packages:**
   - One new client for the 2 Sessions/Week Package + one new client for the 6-Week Challenge
   - Package:
     - $5,200 + $997 = $6,197 (exceeds $4,000 goal)

Achieve a 100% ROI

- **Investment:** $2,000 (for marketing and advertising)
- **Revenue Needed for 100% ROI:** $2,000 x 2 = $4,000

By generating $4,000 in revenue, you meet your 100% ROI goal, effectively doubling your investment.

CHAPTER 9

A GOOD PROBLEM TO HAVE: HOW TO HIRE THE RIGHT PEOPLE FOR YOUR EMS BUSINESS

When I first started my EMS training business and opened my first studio, I wasn't aware that I also needed to be an expert in human resources. Like many of you, I started because I was passionate about EMS and the impact it could have on people's lives. But sure enough, once I signed up my first fifty customers, I realized I needed help. And when I reached 150 memberships and the studio was booming, it hit me — this phase is about team building and leadership. But here's the thing: I didn't have a degree in HR or know much about onboarding processes at the time. How do you lead people?

It's a good problem to have because it means your business is growing, but at the same time, hiring people can be demanding. Looking back, I always jokingly said I should write a book about all the losses and disappointments I experienced when hiring the wrong people. I mean, I did not just hire someone. I put my heart into these people, the same way I did with my clients. I educated and invested in them. Yet, some of these people ended up stealing money, clients, and my concept from me. Many of my former EMS trainers tried to start their own EMS business, but sadly, not often in an ethical way.

And that's why it's crucial to understand how to hire the right people, and that's what I'm here to share with you.

LEARNING FROM EXPERIENCE

Over the years, I've hired some amazing people. These are individuals I still have great relationships with today, and I've watched them grow in ways that have been truly inspiring. They've become a part of my life, and I've become a part of theirs. This business has transformed not only my life but also theirs. But — there's always a but — I've also hired people who weren't the right fit.

I've hired people who doubted EMS, people who were just looking for a job, and even people who showed red flags like not being entirely honest, having attitude problems, not being sales-driven, having many limiting beliefs, being entitled, or not being team players — but I hired them anyway because I felt I had no choice, as there were not enough options in the market. Some, with a lot of education and training, could be transformed into decent trainers, but others were a huge loss to my EMS business.

Bringing someone on board meant a huge investment. For example, I hired a trainer for our team in Qatar. We brought her all the way from Eastern Europe (Bulgaria). She asked if she could bring her husband and if we could help find him a job too. We were in such desperate need of a female EMS trainer that we agreed. We bought their flight tickets, paid for their one-year business visa, certified her, and provided accommodation. After a few weeks, she disclosed to me that she wasn't happy with her furnished accommodation. She asked me if we could provide her with a loan so she could buy furniture and move to another apartment with her husband. We also found her husband a job, but she was complaining about it. She didn't like the conditions of it. We granted her the loan, and she was gone.

I was so upset. All the money, all the effort, hours of re-cruiting, scouting, and educating for nothing. But I was most upset with myself. I should have sent her home the moment I saw her. She didn't look like the healthy person in the pictures on her CV. She was smoking and drinking diet cola nonstop. She looked underweight and turned out to be bulimic. How did I overlook that in the process? The thing is, if you're not equipped with the right steps, tools, and onboarding processes, hiring becomes a game of luck. Sometimes you hit the target, and sometimes you don't.

That's why I developed a step-by-step guide and system-ized my onboarding process. This process ensures that the wrong people filter themselves out early on, allowing you to invest your time, education, and money in someone who can truly grow with you and your brand.

HIRE PEOPLE WHO BELIEVE IN EMS

Here's what I've learned: You need to hire people who are as obsessed and excited about EMS as you are. People who genuinely believe in the product and who either have the know-how or are open and willing to learn how to provide top-notch results for your niche clients.

It's also crucial that they're mentally strong. In business, challenges will arise — it's inevitable. You don't want people who quit or become passive when faced with obstacles. Instead, you need solution-finders, people who see problems and immediately think of ways to overcome them. That's what being in customer service and working in daily EMS operations requires — constantly finding solutions, not focusing on problems.

And let's not forget, they need to love sales. They need to enjoy working with people, transforming lives, and tackling objections clients may have. This process is at the core of running an EMS business. Whether it's booking people in, getting them to show up, signing them up, or keeping them as clients — these are the key activities that will drive your success. If someone has limiting beliefs around sales, it's not impossible to help them overcome that, but it's tough and takes time. You can teach someone how to correct a squat or lunge much faster than you can change their mindset around sales. So, make sure you hire the right people with the right mindset from the beginning.

CULTURE IS EVERYTHING

Another thing I've learned is that if you hire even one negative person, it can affect your entire team. Think of it like a glass of water — one grain of salt is enough to make the whole thing salty. That's why, for the sake of developing a strong, positive culture, you want to hire people who are positive from the get-go. Once you have that strong foundation, you can build great customer service and a successful EMS team.

But before diving into the hiring steps, you need to define your core values. What are your principles? What do you stand for? Having these clearly outlined will help in the decision-making phase. If your core values align with those of the person you're interviewing, it's much easier to determine whether they're the right fit for your team.

At EMS Mastermind, we've developed an EMS trainer assessment and onboarding trial day, together with resources of helpful personality tests to help you understand if a candidate aligns with your organization's culture, values, and mission. It's an extra layer of assurance before you make a hiring decision.

EDUCATE AND ONBOARD

Since EMS is still a relatively new field, you're going to run into the challenge that applicants, much like your prospects, may not know what EMS is. That's why it's so important to have an onboarding process that includes educating your new hires on what electro-muscle stimulation is and how it works.

Once you've started hiring — whether it's one person or multiple people — you need to hold regular team meetings. These meetings foster teamwork, communication, and collaboration among your trainers, ensuring that you're delivering cohesive and effective training sessions to your clients.

ONGOING DEVELOPMENT AND ACCOUNTABILITY

It's also crucial to implement performance evaluations and hold your team accountable for their weekly efforts. I held team meetings every week with my staff, and it was honestly one of my favorite things to do. Our agenda always started with appreciation and new information. We'd spend time on education — whether it was about training skills, mobilization, or EMS methodologies. Every week, we focused on self-development and fine-tuning our processes to ensure the best results for our clients.

A key part of these meetings was also having each team member take responsibility for their numbers and predict their goals for the week ahead. Recognizing their efforts, setting goals, and giving them a sense of ownership over their progress increased engagement and helped foster a strong, motivated team.

CREATE A CLEAR CAREER PATH

It's important that your team doesn't feel like they've hit a ceiling after reaching a certain point in your business. From the beginning, make it clear that there are career paths within your organization and that there are opportunities for growth beyond just being an EMS trainer. This will keep them motivated and hungry for more.

Retention incentives are another way to keep your top EMS trainers. Competitive compensation, benefits, and incentives go a long way in minimizing turnover. The better you take care of your team, the more likely they are to stick around and contribute to your long-term success.

Our 8-Step Team Building Framework

Fig. 4. *8-Step Team Building Framework*

WHAT I KNOW TODAY

Hiring the right people for your EMS business isn't easy, but with the right tools, processes, and mindset, you can build a team that not only believes in your vision but also helps you achieve it. If you'd like access to our success course, with all eight steps and the documents you need to hire the right people, just scan this QR code!

Scan me!

CHAPTER 10

SHIFT YOUR MINDSET FROM TRAINER TO BUSINESS OWNER

Just like your clients, you can't move forward unless you're willing to invest and do the work.

Who you believe you are plays a crucial role in building and growing your EMS business. If you start with limiting "I am" statements, such as, "I am just an EMS trainer" or "I am not a good business owner," it will affect your feelings, actions, and ultimately, your business's outcome. Your identity holds incredible power, and it's vital to shift that identity to match your vision of success.

For example, if you think, "I am a trainer," you'll act differently than if you believe, "I am an EMS business owner developing one of the most successful EMS brands." This shift starts with an internal transformation. Adopting the mindset of a business owner, rather than just a trainer, is essential. Many of us began with a passion for training, a passion for health and fitness and helping others to transform their lives, but that can hold us back from taking the necessary steps to run a thriving business.

Have you ever been in a situation where you want to help someone so much that you offer one-on-one sessions for the price of semi-private sessions? Or do you turn a blind eye to their cancellation ten minutes before class and still let them reschedule even when their class is over?

As a trainer, you can let this slide, thinking, "This is okay; it helps the client," but as an EMS business owner, you know this is harming your business.

Here's a table comparing the mindset, feelings, actions, and outcomes of someone who identifies as "just an EMS trainer and coach" versus someone who sees themselves as an "EMS business owner."

EMS Trainer and Coach	EMS Business Owner
I Am Statement: "I am just an EMS trainer and coach."	**I Am Statement:** "I am an EMS business owner of a brand that will make an impact in my city."
Thoughts & Beliefs: "My job is to help clients get fit."	**Thoughts & Beliefs:** "I am building a brand that transforms lives and grows a thriving business."
Feelings Produced: Limited, underappreciated, dependent on others for success.	**Feelings Produced:** Empowered, motivated, visionary, responsible for own success.
Actions Taken: Focuses solely on delivering training sessions; lacks business development; relies on referrals and word-of-mouth.	**Actions Taken:** Proactively develops the business; invests in marketing, networking, and strategic growth; builds a strong brand presence.
Outcome: Struggles to grow; limited client base; income plateaus.	**Outcome:** Business expansion; brand recognition; steady growth in clients and revenue; a leader in the local EMS industry.

This shift from a limited to an expansive mindset can lead to significant changes in business success and personal fulfillment.

Fig. 5. *Thought-feeling-action-outcome*

So, ask yourself: How do you see yourself, as a trainer or as a business owner? Your mindset and beliefs shape your actions, including your belief in your vision. Do you see your EMS business making an impact in your neighborhood, city, country, or even globally? A clear, compelling vision and commitment to growth are essential.

Change can be uncomfortable, but it's also necessary for growth. As an EMS business owner, your focus expands beyond just training; it encompasses the entire operation. This shift in perspective helps you prioritize what's truly important. Cultivating an entrepreneurial mindset, characterized by innovation and resourcefulness, is key.

Remember, success isn't achieved alone. Surround yourself with like-minded individuals who can provide guidance, resources, and inspiration. Growing your business also means investing in yourself — your time, money, and energy. Financial investment in areas like personal development, sales, hiring staff, marketing, and infrastructure is essential.

The biggest hurdles? Fear-driven patterns like procrastination and perfectionism. These can delay action or prevent you from starting. Taking consistent, daily actions, scheduling them, and staying persistent are the cornerstones of success. Building a successful EMS business isn't about luck; it's about sacrifice, discipline, and the willingness to invest your resources in your vision.

PLAN STRATEGICALLY

Each day, start by reviewing your business goals and setting clear priorities. This simple practice will help you align your daily tasks with the long-term vision you have for your EMS training business. If your goal is to expand your client base, for instance, focus your day on activities like marketing, engaging with clients, or networking. By consistently evaluating key metrics, such as client retention rates and revenue targets, you'll not only ensure your business stays on track but also be able to make timely adjustments to your strategy when needed.

ENGAGE CLIENTS

Client relationships are at the heart of your EMS training business. Make it a daily habit to personally engage with your clients. Whether through emails, phone calls, or quick messages, check in with them to ensure they're happy with their progress and address any concerns or feedback they might have. For new clients, take the time to conduct initial consultations, assess their fitness goals, and create personalized training plans. Depending on the size of your business, you may either lead EMS sessions yourself or closely oversee your trainers to ensure the highest level of service is consistently delivered.

DEVELOP YOUR EMS BUSINESS

Growing your EMS training business requires daily focus and proactive steps. Each day, work on creating and managing marketing campaigns that not only attract new clients but also keep your current ones engaged. This could mean developing compelling social media content, sending out email newsletters, or launching special promotions. Don't overlook networking, either. Attend local business events, industry conferences, or virtual sessions to build valuable relationships and partnerships. Lastly, make sure your brand stays consistent and professional across all platforms, reinforcing your business's image and reputation at every touchpoint.

MANAGE YOUR TEAM

Effectively managing your team is key to the success of your EMS training business. Make it a daily priority to support and develop your EMS trainers. This could include providing ongoing training to keep everyone up-to-date with the latest industry trends and techniques. Weekly or biweekly team meetings help you align on goals, address challenges, and identify areas for improvement. As the leader, you also play a vital motivational role, fostering a positive and productive work environment by offering encouragement and support to your team every step of the way.

MANAGE YOUR FINANCES

As an EMS training business owner, maintaining your financial health is a daily priority. This means regularly reviewing your budget, tracking expenses, and managing cash flow to ensure profitability. Stay on top of client payments, handle necessary financial transactions, and make sure your income aligns with your business goals. Daily financial planning is essential as well — whether it's considering investments in new equipment, launching marketing campaigns, or exploring opportunities for expansion. This constant attention to your finances ensures the long-term growth and stability of your business.

ENHANCE YOUR CLIENTS' EXPERIENCE

Enhancing the client experience is an ongoing commitment. Every day, look for ways to elevate the services you provide — whether it's by adopting the latest EMS technologies, improving customer service, or offering additional value like nutrition counseling. Gathering and analyzing client feedback should be a regular part of your routine, giving you insights into where improvements can be made. By consistently refining your offerings, you ensure that your business stays client-focused and meets their evolving needs.

EDUCATION AND PERSONAL DEVELOPMENT

Staying informed and continuously learning is crucial to your success. Dedicate time each day to keeping up with the latest industry research, trends, and advancements in EMS and fitness training. This might involve reading industry journals, attending webinars, or taking coaching courses. By investing in your personal development, you ensure that you remain knowledgeable and capable of effectively leading your business.

STAY ORGANIZED WITH DAILY ADMINISTRATIVE TASKS

To keep your EMS training business running smoothly, daily administrative tasks are essential. Managing or overseeing the scheduling of client sessions and staff shifts ensures that your operations stay well-organized. Compliance with regulations and adherence to safety protocols is a priority, as is making sure that your business meets all legal requirements by conducting regular safety checks. Maintaining accurate records, such as client progress reports, financial transactions, and operational data, is another key responsibility, keeping everything on track and transparent.

EMBRACE INNOVATION TO STAY COMPETITIVE

In the fast-paced EMS industry, staying competitive means embracing innovation daily. As an EMS business owner, you're constantly brainstorming and researching new opportunities for growth. Whether it's introducing new services, entering new markets, or forming strategic partnerships, your focus on expansion keeps your business thriving. Staying agile and adapting to market changes, client needs, or evolving industry regulations ensures that your business not only keeps up but stays ahead of the curve.

PRIORITIZE SELF-CARE TO SUSTAIN SUCCESS

As a successful EMS training business owner, you understand the importance of self-care. Each day, you set aside time for personal health and well-being, whether it's through regular exercise, healthy eating, or relaxation techniques. Maintaining a healthy work-life balance prevents burnout and ensures that you have the energy and focus to run your business effectively over the long term. By making self-care a priority, you not only sustain yourself but also build a thriving business that meets client needs, achieves financial goals, and maintains a strong market presence.

CHAPTER 11

5 WAYS WE CAN HELP YOU

As I look back at my journey, from building EMS studios to pivoting my focus toward supporting studio owners globally, I've realized one thing: Success isn't just about having the right equipment or the best trainers. It's about creating a business that's sustainable, scalable, and profitable. That's why I've developed a range of services designed specifically to help EMS entrepreneurs like you navigate the challenges of growing your business so you can spend more time doing what you love and less time worrying about the day-to-day operations.

Here are the five core services we provide to help you build and grow your EMS business:

1. **Full EMS Business Growth Retainer**
   If you're looking for comprehensive, long-term support to take your studio to the next level, the Full EMS Business

Growth Retainer is for you. Over the course of twelve months, we provide everything you need to optimize and scale your operations. This includes full access to our CRM app, the EMS Business Academy, and exclusive marketing templates that allow you to streamline your client management, marketing, and operations. Every month, we'll have a one-on-one strategy call to ensure you stay on track, and our weekly group coaching sessions and always-open support chat provide a community where you can learn, share, and grow alongside other like-minded studio owners.

Our goal is to give you the tools and guidance to build a system that works so you can save time and effort while maximizing growth.

2. **Fast-Track Studio Success Program**

For those who are looking to make rapid improvements, our Fast-Track Studio Success Program is a three-month intensive program designed to get immediate results. It focuses on the essential elements of client acquisition and team building — two areas where most studio owners struggle. We provide weekly group coaching and monthly one-on-one sessions so that we can focus on the specific needs of your studio, along with access to our proven CRM platform, tailored marketing funnel setups, and paid campaign setup. By the end of the three months, you'll have a clear growth plan, a fully functional client acquisition system, and the knowledge to take your business to new heights.

3. **EMS Brand License Development**

For those who are ready to expand their brand and establish themselves as industry leaders, the EMS Brand License Development program is a twelve-month journey to creating your own EMS brand. This premium package offers weekly one-on-one calls, full CRM app access, and exclusive entry to all our marketing templates and funnels. Plus, you'll have access to live events, where you can network with other top EMS studio owners and industry experts. This program isn't just about running a studio — it's about creating a brand that stands out and sets the standard in the EMS industry.

4. **EMS Mastermind Trainer Certification**

Our EMS Mastermind Trainer Certification program is the perfect solution for anyone looking to become an EMS expert. Over the course of three months, we provide you with the tools, education, and support needed to achieve certification. You'll gain access to certification courses and our supportive community of EMS professionals. This program is a great fit for those who want to elevate their careers and provide top-tier service to their clients.

5. **EMM Retainer Program**

For those who are looking for ongoing support at a more accessible level, the EMM Retainer Program offers incredible value. With monthly group coaching, access to our EMS Business Academy, and an always-open support chat, you'll have all the tools and support you need to continue growing and improving your studio operations. Whether you need help with client management, marketing, or day-to-day operations, this program gives you a reliable support system to keep things running smoothly.

At the end of the day, my mission is to help EMS entrepreneurs not only survive but thrive. By providing you with the tools, strategies, and support you need, my hope is that you'll be able to build a business that reflects your passion and expertise — without the overwhelm.

Thank you for joining me on this journey, and I can't wait to see how your business grows.

Scan the QR code to learn more about us:

ADVANCEMENTS IN EMS TECHNOLOGY

Innovations in Equipment: Exploring the Latest Developments in EMS Devices and Technology

Over the last decade, I have seen significant innovations in electrical muscle stimulation (EMS) systems. Originally, the devices were wired and required wet spraying (water served as a conductor for the electrical current). Training sessions were usually limited to one user at a time. However, advances have led to the emergence of suppliers selling wireless and dry suit systems. Training in smaller groups is also now possible. All of this together improves the experience for the customer as well as the efficiency of the studio.

Recent findings highlight a particular German supplier called kraftwunder in the market. In addition to classic EMS systems, kraftwunder also develops, manufactures, and sells innovative training systems that make use of modulated medium frequency (EMA). The latter is the company's sales and development focus. This focus is crucial because medium-frequency stimulation has been shown to offer greater effectiveness and better results for users, making it a promising path for both trainers and customers.

Unlike EMS suits, the electrical stimulation of EMA suits enables a more physiological activation of muscle cells. Muscle contraction can be triggered directly in the muscle cell and not exclusively via the motor nerve as with conventional EMS. This not only leads to better depth and volume effects but also to a much more pleasant perception of the impulses during training. The technical requirements and power requirements of the modulated medium frequency are significantly more demanding than with classic EMS.

Most existing EMA systems are still connected to a stationary control unit by cables. Through technical innovation, kraftwunder has succeeded in transferring the process to a small power box, without having to accept any performance limitations. The mobile power box can be attached directly to the suit, together with a small battery, without any cables. Dynamic exercises or location-independent training are no longer a problem with the modulated medium frequency. From my own training with low-frequency EMS, I know that you will feel an intense tingling sensation that activates your muscles. The higher electrical frequency of the medium-frequency EMA suits from kraftwunder, on the other hand, is gentler on the nerves, as a direct muscle effect is possible. In addition, the galvanic skin resistance is better overcome.

This significantly reduces the tingling sensation mentioned above, or it only occurs at higher intensity, making training much more pleasant. But the best thing about it is that I have observed faster recovery and an increase in performance and hypertrophy effects. In summary, the modulated medium frequency has the potential to revolutionize the EMS market, and kraftwunder is aiming to take on a pioneering role in this segment and set the quality standards for the coming years.

Constant research and development are intended to maintain and further expand this lead. This new process offers trainers the best possible training results while also being very comfortable. Both are essential for existing studios to retain customers and support them in achieving their goals in the best possible way.

Dry suit middle frequency set from kraftwunder.

LOOKING FOR AN INNOVATIVE AND TRUSTED EMS SUPPLIER?

If you're searching for a reliable EMS provider to take your business to the next level, I highly recommend kraftwunder. They specialize in next-level EMS and EMA solutions, offering a versatile portfolio designed to meet the needs of both in-home users and studio-based businesses.

With kraftwunder, you have access to the newest EMS suits that provide flexibility for a range of settings, whether your focus is on mobile training with in-home suits or equipping your studio with their advanced studio suits. Their technology is designed with both comfort and performance in mind, ensuring that your clients get the most out of their EMS training sessions.

To learn more about kraftwunder and explore how their products can elevate your EMS or EMA services, simply scan the QR code, which will direct you to their dedicated page.

Special Bonus Code: Mastermind50

THANK YOU

First and foremost, I want to give all glory and honor to God. Without Him, nothing is worthy of doing, and all things find their true meaning in Him. His grace has sustained me, guided me, and carried me through every season.

"Unless the Lord builds the house, the builders labor in vain."
— Psalm 127:1 *(NIV)*

This journey is a testimony of His unfailing love and faithfulness. All that I have accomplished is because of His hand upon my life. Thank you, Lord, for being my rock and my strength. To You be all the glory forever.

I would like to express my deepest gratitude to Johann Cabrera Kunhardt, my dear, beloved husband. Thank you for taking care of our little boy, for waking me up at 4:00 a.m. with coffee and water, and for your unwavering encouragement throughout this journey. Your love and support have meant the world to me.

A special thank you to Nicole Gebhardt and the entire Niche Pressworks team, particularly Kim Han, Dena Patton, Michael Hauge, and Kimberly Fallon, for guiding me every step of the way in realizing this book. Your dedication and expertise have been invaluable.

I would also like to thank James Curran for connecting me with Niche Pressworks, and my dear clients, who have encouraged and supported me to write this book. A heartfelt thank you to all of you who helped promote this book and to those who contributed. A special mention to Natalie Hussion and Mark Fisher — thank you for your testimonials and belief in this project.

I extend my gratitude to Fernando Piloto and Toni Weidt from kraftwunder and to Dr. Nick Bauer, whose partnership continues to bring medical credibility to EMS. Your expertise has greatly contributed to this work.

Finally, a big thank you to sports scientist Richard Neidlein from Frankfurt, Germany, whose twenty years of experience as a personal trainer and sports scientist have been instrumental in backing us up through studies, podcasts, and shared knowledge.

Thank you, each and every one of you, for your support and encouragement. This book would not have been possible without you.

EMS
MASTERMIND

GET **MORE** EMS CLIENTS
WITH OUR
$16K VALUE!
ACQUISITION COURSE

- 10 VIDEO LESSONS PLUS BUSINESS DOCUMENTS TO BUILD A THRIVING EMS STUDIO
- FREE ACCESS TO OUR COMMUNITY
- A COMPLETE SYSTEM VALUED AT $16,000
- FRAMEWORKS TO HELP YOU ATTRACT AND CONVERT MORE CLIENTS FAST

WHY YOU NEED THIS COURSE

PROVEN TECHNIQUES FOR CONSISTENT CLIENT GROWTH
HIGH-VALUE TIPS TO STREAMLINE YOUR SALES PROCESS
READY-TO-USE STRATEGIES FOR BOOSTING CONVERSIONS
READY TO GROW YOUR CLIENT BASE? GRAB IT NOW AND
CLAIM YOUR FREE $16K ACQUISITION COURSE

GET STARTED TODAY!

ORDER NOW AND ACCESS THIS EXCLUSIVE COURSE INSIDE!

ABOUT JEMIMA STEINHART

Jemima Regina Steinhart is a wife, mom, and prominent figure in the field of electro-muscle stimulation (EMS), known for her expertise and contributions to advancing the understanding and application of EMS technology and building a thriving EMS training business. With a background in personal fitness training, coaching, mentoring, and economics, Jemima has dedicated her career to exploring innovative methods for optimizing health, fitness, and recovery.

Having earned recognition as a worldwide "EMS Guru," Jemima is revered for her deep knowledge and practical insights into the benefits and applications of EMS in various contexts, from weight loss training to therapeutic rehabilitation. She is the founder of my30minutes (EMS training brand), EMM (Electro Muscle Mastery), and her high-level coaching program EMS Mastermind, an acclaimed EMS business academy platform that provides education, resources, and mentorship to fitness professionals and healthcare practitioners seeking to harness the power of EMS for their clients' benefit.

Jemima's passion for empowering others through education and mentorship is evident in her commitment to hosting expert panels, workshops, and seminars worldwide, where she shares her wealth of knowledge and expertise with a global audience. Her dynamic approach and innovative strategies have earned her a reputation as a thought leader in the field, inspiring countless individuals to explore the transformative potential of EMS in achieving their fitness and wellness goals.

As a sought-after speaker and consultant, Jemima continues to lead the charge in advancing the field of EMS, pioneering new approaches and techniques that push the boundaries of what is possible in fitness, rehabilitation, and human performance enhancement.

Book a free strategy call:

Contact

Website: ElectroMuscleMastery.com
Email: Jemima@EMSMastermind.com
LinkedIn: Jemima Steinhart
Social: @EMSMastermind

APPENDIX A: MASTER CONVERSION

PHASE 1:
FIRST CONNECTION - GETTING THEM BOOKED

Intro Options:

Hey [Prospect Name], it's [Your Name.] You are on my team for the six-week transformation challenge. Text me back your shirt and pant size to have your custom garment ready for you. I have three spots available. Can you make it in at [X] or [Y] time today? Can't wait to see you soon!

Hey [Prospect Name], it's [Your Name], one of the master coaches here at [Company Name]. I saw you're interested in our [Headline from Ads] transformational six-week challenge. We only have [number of spots] left today and tomorrow. Can I book you in for [X] today before all our spots fill up?

Client question and concern:
"What is the cost?" "Is this for me?"

Your answer:
[Name], I understand that cost is a key factor for you. The great thing about EMS training is that it's a time-efficient and highly effective investment in your health. Our pricing reflects the personalized attention and newest EMS technology you'll receive, ensuring you get the results you're after in a fraction of the time. Can I share more details about our flexible plans with you when you are here for your consultation and trial session?

Other Options:
[Name], I understand that cost is a key factor for you. Have you invested in personal training before? Sessions start at $X [Offer a lower fee only if necessary. To calculate, take your long-term upfront offer and divide by the number of sessions. The single rate is what you share as your lowest possible fee.]

More Options:
[Name], I understand that cost is a key factor for you. Our prices and packages are affordable, and we have a money-back guarantee. May I first ask you what your goal is?

Hey, [Name], I understand you might be wondering about the price. While I can't give you a specific number right now, I can assure you that our program is affordable, and we offer a money-back guarantee. The best way to get an exact price is by discussing your goals and having a consultation with you. This way, we can tailor the best package for your needs.

[Name], of course! Let me first explain how the trial session works and the value it provides. During the trial session, we will provide you with a free EMS training session, a free consultation, and all the information about the perfect membership tailored to your goals. Our memberships start at the lowest twenty-four-month weekly rate, which is [insert lowest rate here]. I am available at [X] time. Does that work for you?

Client concern:
"I'm not sure if this is the right thing for me."

I understand your concerns. Can you tell me the main reason you want to do an EMS trial session with us and what your goal is? How can we help you?

Client concern:
"I want to lose weight."

That's great because our EMS training is perfect for weight loss. With EMS, you can expect benefits like stimulating all muscle groups individually and separately, working directly on the muscles with no limit to activation, and activating more than 90% of muscle fibers during each contraction. In just thirty minutes, our workouts are eighteen times more intense than conventional training. Additionally, EMS helps with muscle building, minimum joint load, back pain treatment, and much more.

Client question:
"What exactly is EMS training?"

EMS stands for electro-muscle stimulation, and it's an effective form of training that appeals to a wide range of target groups, including those looking for medical prevention, rehab, beauty and weight loss, and bodybuilding. It involves using impulse currents to make the muscles contract directly, activating the striated skeletal muscles without reaching the organs or the heart. There are no negative side effects for sport-healthy individuals, and it has been recognized as part of classical techniques in physiotherapy since the 1950s. You will absolutely love it and feel energized like never before.

Are you ready to book your trial session?

PHASE 2:
GETTING THEM TO SHOW UP (PRE-QUALIFYING A LEAD):

Client Question:
"Is it worth trying, and will I be uncomfortable showing up?"

[Prospect Name], I completely get it — it can be a bit daunting to try something new. But let me assure you, the first session is all about making you feel comfortable and seeing firsthand the incredible results EMS can deliver. We'll guide you through every step, making sure you feel supported. The first step is always the hardest, but it's also the most rewarding!

> **You:** [Prospect Name], are you planning on traveling soon, or do you have any other commitments that might interfere with starting your fitness journey?

> **Prospective Client:** No, I don't have any immediate travel plans or commitments.

> **You:** [Prospect Name], that is excellent! Are you the decision maker, or do you need to discuss this with your spouse?

> **Prospective Client:** I need to discuss it with my husband/wife.

> **You:** Should we book a trial session for your spouse as well?

> **Prospective Client:** Yes, please.

More Options:

[Prospect Name], do you have any injuries or medical conditions that we should be aware of before starting your EMS training? This information helps us customize your workout plan safely and effectively.

[Prospect Name], on a scale of 1 to 10, how committed are you to completing the six-week challenge? This will help us understand how best to support you throughout the program.

In order to have real-time communication with your prospective clients, we suggest that you always try to have them on a call, if possible, to build a deeper connection. This is crucial to increase the show-up rate.

Additionally, we recommend sending them a video.

Video Script:

Hello, [Prospect Name]. It's [Your Name], one of the coaches here at/the owner of [Company Name]. We are real people and this is our EMS gym [show front door and studio], right across from [landmark]. You are scheduled for your very first EMS trial session experience, so I just wanted to send you this video to introduce myself and let you know we are excited to meet you and introduce you to everyone. Here are three of my favorite benefits of EMS training: 1. Do you know that you will be burning up to 500 kcal? Yes, that's right. 2. Do you know that you will have an afterburn effect up to eight hours after the training, burning up to two to three thousand calories? Yes, that's right, that explains why people have these amazing results with us. 3. Do you know that EMS training releases "feel good" hormones like endorphins? So get ready to leave here feeling like a million dollars. Text me back what size you wear so we can prepare the suit for you. We can't wait to see you soon.

PHASE 3:
GETTING THEM TO SIGN UP

Leading questions:

How are you feeling [after the trial]?
Are you looking for the best price or the most flexible offer?
Can I show you the offer that I think fits best for you?

Prospective Client: Yes, please.

[Show irresistible offers. After going through them, say]: Will we get started? [Wait. Say nothing. Wait for the customer to say yes.]

Client Concern:
"I'm not sure if I'm ready to commit financially and emotionally."

Your answer: [Name], I hear you — committing to something new can be overwhelming, especially when it comes to your health and wellness. Think of it this way: EMS training is an investment in your future self. Whether it's improving your fitness, reducing pain, or boosting your energy, the benefits extend far beyond the sessions. Plus, we offer various packages that suit different needs and budgets, making it easier for you to start without overcommitting.

If your EMS prospect has more concerns, walk them calmly through their objection.

Client Concern:
"I need to think about it."

I completely understand. Making a decision like this is important, and it's natural that you are afraid to make a mistake. But you can't go wrong with EMS training. Can I share some testimonials or success stories from clients who were in a similar position as you?

Transition to keep momentum: Just so you know, we do have a special offer running right now that I'd hate for you to miss out on. It's available for the next [specific time frame, e.g., just today, one week, or until the end of the month], and I'd be happy to reserve a spot for you while you think things over. How about we book you in, and you get your start-up kit; then you can decide which package you'll do.

Close with an open-ended question: Does that sound good to you? Is there anything specific that's on your mind that I can help clarify?

How to Handle Membership Objections

Concerned about unexpected life events like pregnancy, illness, job loss, relocation, or natural disasters that hold your client back from committing long-term?

Let them know: Rest assured, we've got you covered. Our agreements come with flexibility built in.

Pregnancy: If you become pregnant, we can pause your agreement until you're ready to resume.

Health Issues: Should health problems arise, we'll temporarily suspend the agreement until you're back on track.

Job Loss: In the event of job loss, we'll put your agreement on hold until you're financially stable again.

Relocation: If you move beyond a specified distance, we'll cancel the agreement hassle-free.

Natural Disasters: If a natural disaster strikes, your agreement will be paused until normalcy resumes.

If there is any other objection, simply ask, "What is holding you back? What is behind that? Why do you feel this way?"

Remind them: With our flexible approach, you can commit to your EMS fitness journey worry-free, knowing that unexpected circumstances won't derail your progress. Your satisfaction and well-being are our top priorities.

PHASE 4: GETTING THEM TO BRING REFERRALS

Client Concern: "Do I know the benefits of EMS well enough to tell my family and friends?"

You: What benefits do you experience currently since you've started EMS training?

Client: I sleep better. Feel better. Have more energy. Feel more toned. Have less pain. I feel stronger. I have more endurance.

You: You're experiencing the incredible benefits of EMS first-hand, which couldn't make me any happier! Imagine how much your family and friends could gain from this too. I currently have [X] spots left, and I really would love to help people you care about see the same results as you. Do you know three people whose contact information you'd be willing to share? We even offer referral bonuses as a thank-you for spreading the word.

Action: Follow up with them consistently. Ask consistently.

PHASE 5: GETTING THEM TO STAY

It is crucial to track your clients' attendance, measure their results every four to eight weeks, and book time with them for a progress consultation. In these moments, you will be able to confirm their commitment and offer them a follow-up solution (after a short-term package, like a six-week challenge) or even get them to go for a package that offers more EMS training sessions per week.

If you want to get the full progress consultation guide, scan here:

APPENDIX B:
EMS TRAINING MONEY-BACK
GUARANTEE EXAMPLE

At [Your EMS Training Studio], we are confident in the transformative power of our electro-muscle stimulation (EMS) training programs. We believe that with dedication and adherence to our guidance, you will experience significant results, including losing inches, feeling better, gaining strength, and increasing endurance.

OUR GUARANTEE

If you attend all your scheduled training sessions and follow our comprehensive advice, including nutrition and lifestyle recommendations, but do not see any noticeable results, we will offer you a full money-back guarantee.

TERMS AND CONDITIONS:

1. **Attendance:** You must attend all of your scheduled training sessions as per your agreed-upon plan.

2. **Compliance:** You must follow all training, nutrition, and lifestyle advice provided by our trainers and coaches.

3. **Progress Tracking:** Regular progress tracking will be conducted to measure results, including body measurements, strength tests, and endurance evaluations.

4. **Communication:** Maintain open communication with your trainer, discussing any concerns or difficulties immediately to adjust your plan accordingly.

5. **Time Frame:** This guarantee is applicable after a minimum commitment period of [specific time frame, e.g., eight or twelve weeks], to ensure ample time for results to manifest.

How to Claim:

If, after following all the steps and committing fully to the program, you do not see any of the guaranteed results, you can request a refund by contacting our customer service team. We will review your progress reports and adherence to the program before processing your refund.

WHY WE OFFER THIS GUARANTEE:

We are dedicated to your success and are confident in the effectiveness of our EMS training programs. Our goal is to help you achieve your fitness and wellness objectives, and we stand behind our promise to deliver results.

If you have any questions about our guarantee or would like to discuss your fitness goals, please do not hesitate to reach out to us.

Thank you for choosing [Your EMS Training Studio]. We are committed to your success and look forward to helping you transform your life through EMS training.

APPENDIX C:
WARM LEAD SCRIPT

1. Look at their social account and find one or two things to compliment them on. (Don't take more than thirty seconds.)

    DM Ex 1: *"Thank you for the like, I love that picture with your dog. Is that a labradoodle?"*

    DM Ex 2: *"Wow, that reel on your trip to the Caribbean looks amazing!!"*

2. Move on to the next lead and do the same until you hit the daily quota goal you can handle. (**Pro tip: One hundred contacts per day is the sweet spot**)

3. Once they respond, use A-C-A:
    *   **A**cknowledge what they say
    *   **C**ompliment them
    *   **A**sk a leading question

Your guiding principle here is to sound human and conversational. For example:

Lead: *"Yes, he is a labradoodle. His name is Buddy."*

You: *"Wow, you're a labradoodle Mom, AND you're a nurse. You're a supermom! Do you have time to get workouts in?"*

Once they respond, then you can send the offer using this template:

> *"By the way, do you know anybody who is [describe the struggle your lead just shared, or your dream client avatar's struggle] and is looking to [your dream client avatar's outcome] in [month of your challenge]? We are taking on five clients because that's all we have openings for right now. I help [dream client avatars] get [dream client avatar's outcome] without [effort and sacrifice]. It works. I just had [client name] work with me to get [dream client avatar's outcome] even though she [describe the struggle your lead has]. I also had [client name], who [dream client avatar outcome], and it was his first time trying EMS fitness. Does anyone you know come to mind?"*

OUTCOME:

- *Worst case scenario they say no, and we say, "Is there anyone you don't like?"*
- *Best case: "Yes, me"*
- *Nice case: "Yes, my sister would need this."*

Book them for an appointment the same day or the next, and let them know they will be receiving three text messages between now and their appointment.

www.ingramcontent.com/pod-product-compliance
Lightning Source LLC
Chambersburg PA
CBHW071412210326
41597CB00020B/3475